Depression

About the Author

Lynn P. Rehm, PhD, ABPP, obtained his doctorate in Clinical Psychology from the University of Wisconsin – Madison. He has been on the faculties of the Neuropsychiatric Institute at UCLA and the University of Pittsburgh in Psychology and Psychiatry. He recently retired from the Department of Psychology at the University of Houston after 30 years as Professor. His research and clinical interests center around the psychopathology and treatment of depression. He has published widely on his self-management treatment program for depression and on psychotherapy for depression generally. Dr. Rehm continues to be active professionally and is currently President of the Division of Clinical and Community Psychology of the International Association of Applied Psychology.

Advances in Psychotherapy – Evidence-Based Practice

Danny Wedding; PhD, MPH, Prof., St. Louis, MO
(Series Editor)
Larry Beutler; PhD, Prof., Palo Alto, CA
Kenneth E. Freedland; PhD, Prof., St. Louis, MO
Linda C. Sobell; PhD, ABPP, Prof., Ft. Lauderdale, FL
David A. Wolfe; PhD, Prof., Toronto
(Associate Editors)

The basic objective of this series is to provide therapists with practical, evidence-based treatment guidance for the most common disorders seen in clinical practice – and to do so in a "reader-friendly" manner. Each book in the series is both a compact "how-to-do" reference on a particular disorder for use by professional clinicians in their daily work, as well as an ideal educational resource for students and for practice-oriented continuing education.

The most important feature of the books is that they are practical and "reader-friendly:" All are structured similarly and all provide a compact and easy-to-follow guide to all aspects that are relevant in real-life practice. Tables, boxed clinical "pearls", marginal notes, and summary boxes assist orientation, while checklists provide tools for use in daily practice.

Depression

Lynn P. Rehm
Santa Rosa, CA;
Professor Emeritus, Department of Psychology, University of Houston, TX

Library of Congress Cataloging in Publication

is available via the Library of Congress Marc Database under the
LC Control Number 2010926904

Library and Archives Canada Cataloguing in Publication

Rehm, Lynn P.
    Depression / Lynn P. Rehm.

(Advances in psychotherapy-evidence-based practice ; v. 18)
Includes bibliographical references.
ISBN 978-0-88937-326-6

    1. Depression, Mental. 2. Depression, Mental--Treatment.
I. Title. II. Series: Advances in psychotherapy--evidence-based
practice ; v. 18

RC537.R445 2010   616.85'27   C2010-902782-5

© 2010 by Hogrefe Publishing

PUBLISHING OFFICES
USA: Hogrefe Publishing, 875 Massachusetts Avenue, 7th Floor, Cambridge, MA 02139
                Phone (866) 823-4726, Fax (617) 354-6875; E-mail customerservice@hogrefe-publishing.com
EUROPE: Hogrefe Publishing, Rohnsweg 25, 37085 Göttingen, Germany
                Phone +49 551 49609-0, Fax +49 551 49609-88, E-mail publishing@hogrefe.com

SALES & DISTRIBUTION
USA: Hogrefe Publishing, Customer Services Department,
                30 Amberwood Parkway, Ashland, OH 44805
                Phone (800) 228-3749, Fax (419) 281-6883, E-mail customerservice@hogrefe.com
EUROPE: Hogrefe Publishing, Rohnsweg 25, 37085 Göttingen, Germany
                Phone +49 551 49609-0, Fax +49 551 49609-88, E-mail publishing@hogrefe.com

OTHER OFFICES
CANADA: Hogrefe Publishing, 660 Eglinton Ave. East, Suite 119-514, Toronto, Ontario, M4G 2K2
SWITZERLAND: Hogrefe Publishing, Länggass-Strasse 76, CH-3000 Bern 9

Hogrefe Publishing
Incorporated and registered in the Commonwealth of Massachusetts, USA, and in Göttingen, Lower Saxony,
Germany

Printed and bound in the USA
ISBN: 978-0-88937-326-6

Table of Contents

1

Description

1.1   Terminology

The term *depression* may refer to the normal human emotion of sadness that occurs in response to loss, disappointment, failure, or other misfortune. Dictionary definitions refer to the act of, or the state of, being pressed down. Thus, metaphorically, depression is a mood that has been pressed downward by some force. We refer to sadness as feeling "low" or "down." Depression as a form of emotional disorder is a severe and prolonged form of feeling down that is out of proportion to the force pressing on the person. Mood can go in two directions, down and up, and the emotional disorder of mania is an excessive and prolonged period of an elevated mood. Although the focus of this book is depression, it is necessary to talk about both kinds of disorders of mood to place depression in a context among psychiatric disorders.

The mood disorders are made up a complex set of diagnostic criteria, subtypes, and specifiers in the American Psychiatric Association's *Diagnostic and Statistical Manual* (*DSM*), currently in its fourth edition with a text revision (*DSM-IV-TR*; American Psychiatric Association, 2000). The World Health Organization's *International Classification of Diseases* (ICD) also has a complex system for naming and classifying mood disorders. In addition to these two authoritative sources there are a number of other terms and concepts related to the mood disorders that have historic, research or clinical practice importance.

Depression, as a word to describe low spirits, has been in the language for several centuries. An even older term is *melancholy* or *melancholia*, which goes back to Middle English. The word derives from the Greek for black bile or black choler, one of the four humors of the body in ancient physiology. Melancholy represented an excess of black bile, placing the person in an "ill humor." In the earlier editions of the *DSM*, depression was referred to as *depressive reaction* or *depressive neurosis*.

1.2   Definitions

There are various ways to define depression. As a diagnosis in the *DSM* of the American Psychiatric Association, it is one of the more complex categories. To begin with, the diagnostic criteria define mood episodes: **Major Depressive Episode** (MDE), **Manic Episode**, **Hypomanic Episode**, and **Mixed Episode**. See Table 1 for the full set of criteria for MDE. A Manic Episode consists of a

Types of episodes:
– Depressive
– Manic
– Hypomanic
– Mixed

Table 1
Criteria for Major Depressive Episode

A. Five (or more) of the following symptoms have been present during the same period and represent a change from previous functioning; at least one of the symptoms is either (1) depressed mood or (2) loss of interest or pleasure.

Note: Do not include symptoms that are clearly due to a general medical condition, or mood-incongruent delusions or hallucinations.

(1) depressed mood most of the day, nearly every day, as indicated by either subjective report (e.g., feels sad or empty) or observation made by others (e.g., appears tearful). **Note:** In children and adolescents, can be irritable mood.

(2) markedly diminished interest or pleasure in all, or almost all, activities most of the day, nearly every day (as indicated by either subjective account or observation made by others)

(3) significant weight loss when not dieting or weight gain (e.g., a change of more than 5% of body weight in a month), or decrease or increase in appetite nearly every day. **Note:** In children, consider failure to make expected weight gains.

(4) insomnia or hypersomnia nearly every day

(5) psychomotor agitation or retardation nearly every day (observable by others, not merely subjective feelings of restlessness or being slowed down)

(6) fatigue or loss of energy nearly every day

(7) feelings of worthlessness or excessive or inappropriate guilt (which may be delusional) nearly every day (not merely self-reproach or guilt about being sick)

(8) diminished ability to think or concentrate, or indecisiveness, nearly every day (either by subjective account or as observed by others)

(9) recurrent thoughts of death (not just fear of dying), recurrent suicidal ideation without a specific plan, or a suicide attempt or a specific plan for commit; suicide

B. The symptoms do not meet criteria for a Mixed Episode

C. The symptoms cause clinically significant distress or impairment in social, occupational, or other important areas of functioning.

D. The symptoms are not due to the direct physiological effects of a substance (e.g., drug-of abuse, a medication) or a general medical condition (e.g., hypothyroidism).

E. The symptoms are not better accounted for by Bereavement, i.e., after the loss of a loved one, the symptoms persist for longer than 2 months or are characterized by marked functional impairment, morbid preoccupation with worthlessness, suicidal ideation, psychotic symptoms, or psychomotor retardation.

distinct period of elevated, expansive, or irritable mood that lasts at least one week (less if hospitalization is required). In addition, three of the following symptoms are necessary (four if mood is irritable): inflated self-esteem or grandiosity; decreased need for sleep; more talkative than usual; flight of ideas or racing thoughts; distractibility; increase in goal-directed activity; and excessive involvement in pleasurable activities. The episode is Manic if it leads to impairment in functioning or necessitates hospitalization to prevent harm to self or others. If the same criteria are met for at least four days but the impairment criterion is not met, then it is a Hypomanic Episode. Mixed Episode, as the name implies, has mixed symptoms of depression and mania and the criteria for both episodes are met. People in Mixed Episodes describe the feeling as being "wired," i.e., they report being uncomfortably agitated and unable to sit still.

The history of episodes is then examined to determine the diagnosis. If only MDEs have been present, the diagnosis is **Major Depressive Disorder** (MDD). If one or more Manic Episodes has occurred, the diagnosis is **Bipolar I Disorder**. If one or more MDEs and one or more Hypomanic Episodes have occurred with no full Manic Episode, then **Bipolar II Disorder** is the diagnosis. Although it is not in the *DSM*, some researchers and clinicians also refer to **Bipolar III Disorder**. If only MDEs have occurred, but there is a family history of Bipolar Disorder, the person might be diagnosed Bipolar III. The implication is that this person would be better treated with medications targeting Bipolar Disorder. Medications targeting MDD may produce manic episodes in people with underlying Bipolar Disorder (I, II, or III).

Diagnoses depend on the history of episodes

MDD is diagnosed as either **Single Episode** or **Recurrent**. Further, if the current episode meets the full criteria, it can be further described by the following episode specifiers (Table 2): (1) Mild, Moderate, Severe With Psychotic Features, or Severe Without Psychotic Features; (2) Chronic; (3) With Catatonic Features; (4) With Melancholic Features; (5) With Atypical Features; and (6) With Postpartum Onset. If the full criteria are not met by the current episode, it can be specified as In Partial Remission or In Full Remission along with any of 2 through 6 above.

The severity rating of episodes is a recognition that depression is dimensional within the categorical system of the *DSM*. Instruments for measuring severity will be covered later in this chapter. Although the *DSM* lists sets of criteria for deciding whether a person should receive a particular diagnosis or fit into a category, these criteria are polythetic in that not all criteria must be met by any individual and different individuals may meet the criteria with

Table 2
Episode Specifiers

Severity Specifiers
  Mild
  Moderate
  Severe With Psychotic Features
  Severe Without Psychotic Features

Episode Specifiers
  Chronic
  With Catatonic Features
  With Melancholic Features
  With Postpartum Onset

Remission Specifiers
  In Partial Remission
  In Full Remission

different patterns of criterion symptoms. The system has also been referred to as prototypic (Cantor, Smith, French, & Mezzich, 1980), in that the full set of criteria define the prototype, i.e., the complete and full form of the disorder. A particular individual who has a minimal subset of these criteria is considered a sufficient match to the prototype. Natural language is prototypic. When we use the word "chair," the mental prototype has a seat, four legs, and a back, but we recognize many other objects as a sufficient match to call them a chair, such as a chair with fewer legs, or even a "bean bag chair." The boundaries are fuzzy. How wide does a chair have to be to become a couch? Psychiatric diagnoses are similarly fuzzy with marginal cases, overlaps, and indefinite boundaries.

A diagnosis is a sufficient match to a prototype

Severe depression can have **Psychotic Features**, including delusions, hallucinations, and other positive and negative signs usually associated with **Schizophrenia**. Delusions during episodes of depression are most often "mood congruent," i.e., they are characterized by themes of guilt, punishment, disease, or decay with negative meaning for the patient. They may be bizarre or nonbizarre. Bizarre delusions are concerned with ideas that are not possible, e.g., the person is rotting away inside. Nonbizarre delusions can also occur, e.g., a woman may believe she is being poisoned because of her sinful behavior. Manic Episodes may also have psychotic features. Delusions are typically mood congruent and may be bizarre, e.g., a man may believe he has magical powers, or nonbizarre, e.g., a woman may be convinced she has wonderful ideas for a new TV show and must find a way to share her idea with a famous TV personality. The **Chronic** episode specifier is used when a depressive episode lasts for a minimum of 2 years with the criteria continuously met.

Depressive and Manic Episodes may be psychotic

Catatonic Features are similar to the characteristics seen in **Schizophrenia, Catatonic Type**. Most frequently this condition is characterized by motoric immobility or stupor, extreme negativism and resistance to instructions, mutism, inappropriate posturing, and echolalia (repeating meaningless phrases or echoing back what others say) or echopraxia (mimicking others' gestures). Individuals in such a state may stay in uncomfortable positions that can be altered by others in what is known as "waxy flexibility," i.e., flexible like a wax statue. Alternatively, the person may show excessive agitated motor activity that is purposeless and not influenced by external stimuli (American Psychiatric Association, 2000).

Depression can be catatonic

Historically, a distinction was made between reactive or exogenous depressions and endogenous depressions. The basic idea behind this distinction is that some depressions occur as a response or reaction to loss or other environmental stress, whereas other depressions occur without a precipitating event and are thought to have an internal, endogenous origin. The former were assumed to be treatable by psychotherapy, whereas the latter, being of biological origin, were better treated by medication. However, this distinction was difficult to apply with any reliability. As clinicians learn more about individual patients over time, they are more likely to identify precipitating events to which the patients were reacting. Thus, low reliability has led to a decline in the use of the distinction. **With Melancholic Features** follows in this tradition, but without reference to etiology. Persons with these characteristics are still typically assumed to have a more biological form of depression, that is better treated with medication. The primary characteristic of melancholic depression is a

Melancholic depressions are assumed to have a more biological origin

loss of pleasure in all or almost all activities, or a lack of reactivity to usually pleasurable stimuli. This characteristic is also referred to as *anhedonia*—the lack of the ability to experience pleasure. In addition, melancholic depression has three or more of the following characteristics: (1) a distinct quality of depressed mood (experienced as something different from ordinary sadness or grief); (2) depression that is regularly worse in the morning; (3) early morning awakening (a form of insomnia defined as waking at least 2 hours before one's usual time of waking); (4) marked psychomotor retardation or agitation; (5) significant anorexia or weight loss (without attempting to diet); and (6) excessive or inappropriate guilt (American Psychiatric Association, 2000). We will come back to Melancholic depression and the implications of the concept for treatment in a later chapter.

Typical depression involves loss of appetite and weight and difficulty sleeping. **With Atypical Features** implies increase in appetite, weight gain, and excessive sleeping. Technically, the criteria include first, mood reactivity (in contrast to the anhedonia of Melancholic depression), and second, two or more of the following: (1) significant weight gain or increase in appetite; (2) hypersomnia; (3) leaden paralysis (heavy, leaden feeling in arms or legs); and (4) a long-standing pattern of interpersonal rejection sensitivity that results in significant social or occupational impairment (American Psychiatric Association, 2000).

> Atypical depressions involve increase in appetite, weight, and sleep

With Postpartum Onset is diagnosed when the onset of the episode is within 4 weeks of giving birth. Postpartum depression was once generally thought to be a separate form of biologically caused depression. Today the etiology is seen as more complex, and postpartum depression is classified as a specific form of the disorder within the mood diagnoses.

> Postpartum depressions are now seen as a subset of Major Depressive Disorder

In addition to the episode specifiers above, the *DSM* lists three course specifiers: (1) **With/Without Interepisode Recovery**, i.e., whether full remission is obtained between episodes; (2) **Seasonal Pattern,** a regular association between the onset of episodes and time of the year; and (3) **Rapid Cycling**, whether the person with a Bipolar I or II diagnosis has four or more distinct mood episodes in a year, separated by full remission.

> Course Specifiers: With/Without Interepisode Recovery Seasonal Pattern Rapid Cycling

Seasonal Pattern may be seen in MDD, Bipolar I, or Bipolar II disorders. Typically it involves the regular onset of episodes of depression in the fall and remission or switch to mania in the spring. More rarely, manic episodes may have a spring onset and Fall Remission.

In addition to these major mood disorders, the *DSM* also identifies **Dysthymia** under the depressive disorders and **Cyclothymia** under the bipolar disorders. These are lesser, but more chronic versions of depression and bipolar disorder. Dysthymia requires a duration of two years during which the person has depressed mood "most of the day, more days than not" (APA, p. 380), but only two of a list of six symptoms. Cyclothymia also requires a duration of 2 years, during which the person must have had numerous periods of hypomanic and depressed symptoms that never meet criteria for either episode. Dysthymia has specifiers of **Early Onset** (before age 21) or **Late Onset** (after age 21), and **With Atypical Features** (defined the same as with Major Depression). Early Onset Dysthymia may be continuous from childhood, and thus bears some resemblance to a personality disorder. Psychological approaches to treatment reflect this similarity and will be addressed in a later chapter.

> Dysthymia and Clyclothymia are chronic milder versions of unipolar and bipolar disorders

The *DSM* also has an appendix entitled "Criteria sets and axes provided for further study." As implied, these categories have been suggested by various authorities, but have not been formally adopted by the *DSM* committees pending further research using the proposed criteria to establish their validity. These include **Depressive Personality Disorder** heavily based on psychological symptoms such as gloom, negative self-esteem, and pessimism, in contrast to the more biologically based symptoms sets of Dysthymia and Major Depressive Disorder. **Minor Depressive Disorder**, on the other hand, uses the same nine-symptom set, but requires a minimum of only two (but less than five) symptoms (i.e., less than Major Depressive Disorder). **Recurrent Brief Depressive Disorder** requires that criteria for a Major Depressive Episode are met, except for the 2 week duration criterion. The person must have at least one of these episodes per month for a year. **Mixed Anxiety-Depressive Disorder**, as the name implies, involves a symptom list that includes both anxiety and depression symptoms without meeting criteria for either type of specific diagnosis.

The *DSM* is based on a categorical view of psychiatric disorders. Thus, issues of severity are dealt with in part with severity specifiers, but also by creating separate categories for fewer symptoms or for shorter duration than are required for the primary diagnoses. For example, Dysthymia and Minor Depressive Disorder have fewer symptoms and Recurrent Brief Depressive Disorder is defined by brief duration. A more psychological perspective might see depression as dimensional in terms of severity and perhaps duration as well. The *DSM* categorical view leads to such oddities as the concept of "double depression," a term used to describe a person who has first met criterion for Dysthymia and then qualifies for a Major Depressive Disorder. Under the *DSM* categorical system, the person can be given both diagnoses, thus "double depression." Another oddity occurs when symptoms of two disorders overlap and the overlap is given a separate category name, as in Mixed Anxiety-Depressive Disorder. Another example in the *DSM* is **Schizoaffective Disorder**, which is diagnosed when a Major Depressive Episode occurs while symptoms of Schizophrenia are met.

The World Health Organization publishes the *International Statistical Classification of Diseases*, now in its tenth revision, commonly referred to as the *ICD-10* (World Health Organization, 1992). Its purpose is to support the classification and tabulation of morbidity and mortality data from around the world. In the United States, the National Center for Health Statistics produces a "Clinical Modification," known as the *ICD-10-CM*, for the purpose of classifying and tabulating incidence and prevalence of diseases and disorders in the US. Effort is made to coordinate the *ICD-10-CM* system with US diagnostic codes, such as those in the *DSM*. With regard to the mood disorders, slightly different terms are applied and diagnoses are grouped somewhat differently, but for the most part diagnoses are similar. The major categories in the *ICD-10-CM* are identified in Table 3. Within the first four categories are subtypes based largely on severity. **Persistent Mood Disorders** include Dysthymia and Cyclothymia. The *ICD-10* system is an important alternative system to the *DSM* and is used in many places in the world instead of the *DSM*.

At the time of this writing, the revision processes are underway for both the *DSM-V*, due in 2014, and the ICD-11, due in 2012. A number of changes

---

New diagnostic criterion sets are provided in the DSM to promote further study

Depression overlaps with anxiety and schizophrenic diagnoses

The ICD-10 is a diagnostic system published by the World Health Organization

ICD diagnoses are somewhat different than DSM diagnoses

Table 3
Major Categories of Disorders in the *ICD-10-CM*

Manic Episode

Bipolar Affective Disorder

Depressive Episode

Recurrent Depressive Disorder

Persistent Mood (affective) Disorders (Dysthymia and Cyclothymia)

Other Mood (affective) Disorders

are expected. An initial goal of basing the *DSM* more heavily on biological markers was determined to be premature (Frances, 2009). The *DSM* groups are planning on adding dimensional components to diagnoses, paying more attention to developmental and cultural issues, and coordinating diagnoses with the ICD system. The ICD is expected to pay greater attention to daily functioning and quality of life (Kupfer, Regier, & Kuhl, 2008).

Both the DSM and ICD are being revised

The various diagnoses described above are relevant to assessment and treatment of depression. However, depression as emotion per se is also relevant to understanding the phenomena of depression. There is a long research tradition of studying the relationships among the emotional connotations of words. The classic work was done by Charles Osgood (1962) using the technique of the semantic differential in which affective words are rated on a series of bipolar dimensions. Osgood established that connotation could be accounted for by the three primary dimensions of evaluation (good–bad), potency (strong–weak), and activity (active–passive).

Since Osgood's work, a number of different models have been developed to account for the basic dimensions of emotion. Prominent among these is Russell's (1980) two-dimensional circumplex model that arranges emotions around a circle like colors in a color wheel. The horizontal and vertical axes of Russell's model are pleasure–displeasure (happy–sad) and arousal (tense–relaxed). Depression is located at the extreme end of the horizontal displeasure dimension and at a virtual neutral point on the arousal dimension.

Basic conceptions of emotion inform our understanding of depression

A similar circumplex was described by Watson and Tellegen (1985). The Watson and Tellegen model can be construed as a 45-degree rotation of Russell's model, but it adds the intriguing element of suggesting that the primary horizontal and vertical axes of the circumplex are positive and negative affect as separate and independent dimensions rather that opposite poles of a single dimension. In this model, depression is represented by high negative affect and a relative absence of positive affect. On the basis of this model, the authors (Watson, Clark, & Tellegen, 1988) developed an instrument for assessing positive and negative affect, the Positive Affect Negative Affect Scale (PANAS), which will be reviewed later in the chapter. Clark and Watson (1991) presented a model of anxiety and depression that added a third dimension. In this case, the dimensions are identified as general distress (negative affect), anhedonia (lack of positive affect), and physiological hyperarousal, which is akin to Osgood's potency. These models help define the emotion of depression and are relevant to understanding the mechanisms by which psychotherapy of depression works.

1.3   Epidemiology

Depression is often referred to as the common cold of mental illness because of its high prevalence. The World Health Organization ranks depression as the fourth largest global burden of disease based on years lived with disability (World Health Organization, 1992). Over the last few decades, several large-scale epidemiological studies have assessed the prevalence of depression and other disorders in the United States and in the world. In the late 1980s, the National Institute of Mental Health (NIMH) Epidemiological Catchment Area study results were published (Regier et al., 1988). This study analyzed community samples from five catchment areas around the US: New Haven, Baltimore, St. Louis, Durham, and Los Angeles. The study reported 6-month and lifetime prevalence of all affective disorders as 5.8% and 8.3%. For a manic episode, the figures were 0.5% and 0.8%; for a major depressive episode they were 3.0% and 5.8%; and for dysthymia they were 3.3% and 3.3%. Affective disorder rates were second only to anxiety disorder rates. Women had a 1-month prevalence rate of 6.6% compared to 3.5% for men.

Results of the National Comorbidity Study were published in 1994 (Kessler et al., 1994). This study interviewed a national stratified probability sample of noninstitutionalized individuals aged 15 to 54. Rates for any affective disorder were lower than for any anxiety disorder and for substance-abuse disorders. Twelve-month and lifetime prevalence of 11.3% and 19.3% for any affective disorder were reported. For manic episode, the rates were 1.3% and 1.6% (women 1.3% and 1.7%, men 1.4% and 1.6%); for major depressive episode they were 10.3% and 17.1% (women 12.9% and 21.3% and men 7.7% and 12.7%); and for dysthymia they were 2.5% and 6.4% (women 3.0% and 8.0% and men 2.1% and 4.8%).

Most recently, the National Comorbidity Study has been replicated (NCS-R) in a national face-to-face interview survey of a probability sample of respondents age 18 and older. This survey yielded a 12-month and lifetime rate of MDD of 6.6% and 16.2% (Kessler et al., 2003). Bipolar I disorder was found to have 0.6% and 1.0% prevalences; Bipolar II was 0.8% and 1.1%, and subthreshold Bipolar was 1.4% and 2.4% (Merikangas et al., 2007). Overall, the reported 12-month and lifetime prevalences of mood disorders was 9.5% and 20.8% (Kessler et al., 2005; Kessler, Chiu, Demler, Merikangas, & Walters, 2005). Statistics vary among studies because of minor differences in instruments used, training of interviewers, participation rates, and other factors, along with random error. Rates of MDD are consistently higher than either bipolar or dysthymia, and women have consistently higher rates of MDD.

1.3.1   Age Cohort

One of the interesting findings in the NCS-R study (Kessler et al., 2003) arose from the interviewers asking participants the age of onset of their first episode of depression while determining lifetime prevalence. Data were plotted for age cohorts of age 60 or greater, 45–59, 30–44, and 18–29. These curves are progressively steeper, i.e., the younger you are the earlier the onset of your first episode of depression and the higher the probability that you will have an episode in your lifetime. From their graph, a total of about 13% of 60+ year olds reported lifetime depression, and just over 20% of 45–59 year olds, 24% of 30–44 year olds, and about 25% of 18–29 year olds reported depression already in their lifetime.

This is not a new finding. Very similar cumulative graphs were published in 1992 (Cross-National Collaborative Group, 1992). Both participants who were born from 1905 to 1914 (then averaging about 65) and those born before 1905 reported lifetime totals of depressive episodes of about 1%, compared to about 3% for those born from 1915 to 1924, about 5% for 1925 to 1934, about 9% for 1935 to 1944, about 9.5% for 1945 to 1954, and already 6% for 1955 or later (roughly 25 year olds) that also showed the steepest upward curve. With the exception of some Hispanic samples, the same sets of curves were found around the world in nine epidemiological studies and three family studies.

These findings must be interpreted with some caution. Many possible artifacts could be influencing these graphs. Even though participants were asked about times when they experienced specific symptom clusters, older people may be less likely to label their recollections as episodes of depression and may be more likely to forget they had them. Younger people may be more aware of the diagnosis of depression. In succeeding generations, it has become progressively more socially acceptable to identify oneself as depressed. Also, some of the more severely depressed individuals may not have survived into the older age groups.

Despite these caveats, the evidence is too consistent and comes from too many findings to dismiss it. *The more recently you were born the more likely you are to develop depression in your lifetime, and the earlier in your life you are likely to experience a first episode.* Why should this be? Depression has a biological component, but I have not heard anyone suggest that genetics or biology has changed so rapidly in only a few decades. In fact, the increase in depression raises some questions for the biological perspective on depression. Does it mean that the biological predisposition has been carried by a larger segment of the population and stress has simply increased its effect on people? Most people would attribute these dramatic data to changes that have taken place in society.

Martin E. P. Seligman (1990) proposed an answer to the question "Why is there so much depression today?" He proposed that the increase in depression corresponds to changes that have taken place in our society that increase a sense of personal responsibility for negative events, and a similar change in which communities have lost their ability to respond to problems. Seligman

> **Seligman suggests that the stress on individuality in the US is responsible for increased rates of depression**

Clinical Vignette
Self-Diagnosis

An older psychiatrist once told me that he used to see patients who would say "Doctor, I am not sleeping well, I have lost my appetite, and I am really feeling badly about myself." He would reply, "Oh, you must be depressed." He said that today patients say to him, "Doctor, I am depressed," and he says "Oh, are you not sleeping well? Have you lost your appetite and are you feeling badly about yourself?" People today are much more ready to self-diagnose.

suggests that we are living in an "age of the individual" in which our society stresses the responsibility of the person, giving him or her both credit and blame. He attributes this emphasis largely to the prosperity of the United States, which allows individuals to make a wide variety of individual choices in their lives. At the same time he cites a lessening of community responsibility. As our population becomes more mobile and families are fragmented, our sense of belonging to a community decreases. We do not have stable living communities, and communities built around institutions such as schools and churches have lost their power as well. Seligman also sees historic events in the United States as contributing to our sense that society cannot solve its problems. He uses the political assassinations of the 1960s, the Vietnam War, and Watergate to illustrate his point that most people have lost faith in the country's ability to find solutions to problems.

The result is that individuals feel the full weight of responsibility for their choices and for their successes and failures. A child who does poorly in school is seen as a personal failure while the family, the school, and the community take little responsibility for this problem. Individual responsibility makes us more vulnerable to take responsibility for failure and to feel helpless to change our lives. Seligman views helplessness as a central element in depression. His helplessness theory of depression will be reviewed in a later chapter.

Seligman's explanation for the increase in depression focuses on historic events in the United States. However, the phenomenon of increases in the rates of depression is found elsewhere as well (Cross-National Collaborative Group, 1992). Some of the places where increases in depression have been reported (e.g., Italy, Lebanon, Taiwan, and New Zealand) have very different social climates and histories. The sense of individuality, for example, may be less prevalent in Taiwan and in New Zealand. These other countries may also have experienced frustrations with national solutions to problems, but one would not expect these events to coincide with the problems the United States has faced. One problem with Seligman's explanation of the change in society is that it focuses on issues during a particular historic period: the 1960s. If the 1960s were a turning point, then the various cumulative curves for the different age cohorts should become steeper when that cohort was living through that era. Such inflections in the curves are not obvious. If an increase in helplessness and loss of control over our lives is the cause of the increases in depression, it has to be an effect that is gradual and worldwide. The Cross-National Collaborative Group (1992) suggested that empirical studies of how various demographic, epidemiological, economic, and social indices are related to increases in depression in different countries might shed light on the relevant causes.

1.3.2 Gender

Beginning in adolescence, women have higher rates of depression than men

The prevalence of depression is higher among women than among men. The *DSM* (American Psychiatric Association, 2000) cites women/men ratios of between 2:1 and 3:1. The National Comorbidity Survey reported a ratio of about 1.7:1 for both lifetime and 12-month prevalence (Kessler et al., 1994). The NCS-R study found about the same lifetime ratio and a 1.4:1 ratio for 12-month prevalence (Kessler et al., 2003). In contrast, *the rates for Bipolar*

Disorder are approximately equal for men and women. The gender ratios for depression are not limited to the United States. In reviews of the available data, Myrna Weissman and colleagues (Weissman et al., 1996; Weissman & Klerman, 1977) cite data from studies outside the US that document that 1.5 to 2.0 times as many women as men become depressed. Boys and girls score about equally on depression inventories. It is not until adolescence that the scores and rates of depression diverge (Twenge & Nolen-Hoeksema, 2002).

A number of different explanations have been offered for the higher rates of depression in women, including endocrine and hormone hypotheses. Cyranowski and colleagues (Cyranowski, Frank, Young, & Shear, 2000) suggest that pubertal hormones increase affiliative needs in adolescent girls, thereby intensifying socialization stress. Family studies suggest that depression has a heritable component. Several studies, however, have found that depression in women and substance abuse in men (especially alcoholism), run in the same families (Winokur & Clayton, 1967). This suggests a similar underlying genetic component, but men may be discouraged from expressing depression and may medicate their depression with alcohol. Hammen and Peters (1977) demonstrated that both male and female raters were less positive toward a fictitious "fellow student" who had symptoms of depression when that person was given a male name. They concluded that men meet with negative reactions when they display depression and thus learn alternative ways to deal with their negative feelings. Depression is not only more acceptable in women, it may be that women are encouraged by meeting others expectations of depression. One study of family perceptions among adult family members found that women are more likely to be reported as depressed by a member of the family, even when they themselves do not report depression (Brommelhoff, Conway, Merikangas, & Levy, 2004). Family members were also more likely to attribute the depression of women to internal causes, whereas they attributed external causes equally between men and women. This gender bias may lead to women being more susceptible to depression because they are confirming others' impressions of them and others may reinforce these confirmations.

Radloff (1975) reviewed demographic correlates of depression and reported that, among men, *married and divorced men are the least depressed and widowed men are the most depressed.* Among women, *married and divorced women exhibit a higher incidence of depression with never-married the least depressed.* Women are more depressed than men if working, whereas men are more depressed if unemployed. Being young, poor, and having limited education are all correlates of depression, but when controlled for, they do not account for the differences in rates of depression between men and women. When marital and job satisfaction are controlled for, working wives are less depressed than wives who are not working, though still more depressed than working husbands. Radloff interprets these data in terms of a job outside of the home being an outlet for self expression for women. She concludes by drawing on a learned helplessness model of depression, suggesting that women have more constraints on their lives and are more prone to feeling helpless to control outcomes. Greater vulnerability due to a more helpless explanatory style in female children has also been suggested by Nolen-Hoeksema, Girgus, and Seligman (1991).

Sociotropic persons are more susceptible to interpersonal losses, and autonomous persons are more susceptible to achievement-related losses

Aaron Beck (1983) introduced the concept of **sociotropy–autonomy** to explain individual differences in the ways people are vulnerable to depression. A sociotropic individual is focused on interpersonal relationships and bases his or her self-esteem on the good opinion of others. The autonomous person is focused on achievement and goal attainment and finds self-worth in success in these endeavors. Sociotropes are susceptible to depression when interpersonal relationships are disrupted or lost. Autonomous individuals are more susceptible to depression when they encounter a failure or other blows to their achievement goals. Although the concepts are often discussed as if these are two opposite types of people, the scale developed to measure sociotropy–autonomy views them as separate dimensions, such that a person could be high or low on both (Bieling, Beck, & Brown, 2000). Relevant to the difference in depression between men and women is the common finding that women more frequently score high on sociotropy whereas men more frequently score high on autonomy. Women may be more vulnerable than men because of the higher likelihood of interpersonal stresses in our society.

On a similar note, Sidney Blatt and his colleagues (Blatt, Quinlan, Chevron, McDonald, & Zuroff, 1982) drew on a psychodynamic tradition and proposed a distinction between dependent and self-critical experiences of depression. The dependent dimension of depression, once called *anaclitic depression*, is characterized by feelings of helplessness, weakness, and fears of abandonment. Self-critical depression, earlier termed *introjective*, is characterized by feelings of competition, worthlessness, guilt, and constant self-evaluation. Blatt later added a third dimension of efficacy characterized by goal-oriented striving and valuing of accomplishment. Dependent tendencies are similar to sociotropy, whereas Blatt's latter two dimensions are similar to autonomy. This group (Zuroff, Quinlan, & Blatt, 1990) has developed a Depressive Experiences Questionnaire to measure the three dimensions. As with other measures of depression, women tend to score higher on dependency and thus may be more vulnerable to depression based on stresses related to dependent relationships.

Women are more likely to respond to loss with a ruminative coping style

Another answer to the question of why women might have a greater risk for depression is offered by Susan Nolen-Hoeksema (Nolen-Hoeksema, 1987; Nolen-Hoeksema, Larson, & Grayson, 1999) in terms of different coping styles between men and women. In response to an event that brings on sad feelings, women are more likely to respond passively and to ruminate about the event and its causes and implications. They are more likely to discuss their sadness with others and try to find the reasons behind their mood. Men are more likely to respond actively by thinking about something else or distracting themselves with some other activity. While a ruminative coping style is a continuous dimension, such that both women and men may ruminate and both may distract to varying degrees, women score higher on rumination and men score higher on distraction. *Rumination prolongs and amplifies the negative feelings whereas distraction cuts them short.* Rumination also allows time to associate events and reactions to similar events in the past and to develop pessimistic, depressive explanations for personal events. Rumination is seen as interacting with other chronic strains and a low sense of mastery to produce depression.

There is clearly some overlap among these explanations. The sociotropic person may be more dependent on others, fear abandonment, feel helpless, and ruminate about problems in relationships. The autonomous person may over-invest his or her self-esteem in a job and be critical of his or her work. There have also been attempts to develop integrative models incorporating multiple causal factors.

Hyde, Mezulis, and Abramson (2008) present an ABC model that links affective, biological, and cognitive vulnerabilities with life stress. The model incorporates most of the factors cited above and adds a few additional risks for depression to which women are exposed. The affective factors they cite include personality style, dependency and affiliative needs (cf. sociotropy), and temperament, such as negative emotionality. Biological factors include familial risk, specific genetic mechanisms, and pubertal hormones. Cognitive factors include negative cognitive style (helpless attributions), rumination, and body-image dissatisfaction. Beginning in adolescence, all of these interact with stressors such as broadly construed sexual abuse, negative interpersonal events, and pressure to conform to gender roles. The model nicely incorporates factors from theoretical models that have empirical support.

1.3.3   Summary

Depression is a widespread disorder that has a major impact on society. Research suggests that both Major Depression and Bipolar Disorder are on the rise around the world, although the reasons for this are unclear. Children score equally on depression measures, but by adolescence depression is more common among women by about 1.5:1 to 2.0:1. This is true around the world. A number of factors have been proposed to account for these differences and many of them have empirical support.

1.4   Course and Prognosis

The description of mood disorders in the latest version of the *DSM* addressed the course of the disorder in great detail. Course descriptors were written in for the subtypes and specifiers. Single Episode and Recurrent are subtypes. Recurrence is also a significant feature for prognosis. Among people who have a first episode of MDD, 50% experience a second episode, and of those with a second episode, about 70% experience a third episode. People who experience three episodes have a 90% chance of having a fourth and more (American Psychiatric Association, 2000). The course of Recurrent MDD is further described by course specifiers: With, and Without Full Interepisode Recovery; Seasonal Pattern; and Rapid Cycling. Without Full Interepisode Recovery implies that depression can be almost continuous with a waxing and waning course. Because of the probability of recurrence and lack of full recovery between episodes, many experts believe depression should be considered a chronic disorder and treated as such.

The typical age of onset for a first episode of depression is the mid-twenties. As discussed earlier, however, onset is earlier for people born in more

The DSM-IV emphasizes variations in the course of depression

First episodes of depression typically occur in the mid-twenties, but onsets seem to be shifting to earlier ages

recent decades. Depression is being diagnosed more frequently in children as well. Diagnosing children with depression has led to some controversy. The syndrome is less coherent in children and hence the reliability of diagnosis is low. Many children are treated with antidepressant medications even though evidence for the effectiveness of antidepressants in children is sparse. Concern that some selective serotonin reuptake inhibitors (SSRIs) may lead to increased rates of suicide in children and adolescents has led to warning labels on these medications, even though the evidence is controversial.

Seasonal Pattern disorders typically have fall onsets and spring remissions. Nonseasonal disorders have more fall onsets and spring remissions

Seasonal Pattern is clearly related to exposure to light and the length of days. Less light leads to the onset of depression. This type of depression is more common closer to the poles and less common closer to the equator, where there is less variability in annual daylight. The *DSM* requires that this occurs for at least 2 years in a row with seasonal episodes far outnumbering nonseasonal ones. Interestingly, research suggests that, even in individuals who do not show a regular seasonal pattern, there is a higher probability of depressive episode onsets in the fall and remissions in the spring than in other seasons. Seasonal Pattern has only been recognized in recent decades in the *DSM*; however, it is a long-known phenomenon in Scandinavian countries, where it is referred to with terms like "Spring Disease," and where the traditional treatment is to recommend use of sun lamps. Bright light as a treatment for depression will be covered in a later chapter.

Today postpartum depressions are thought of as an episode subtype rather than a separate disorder

Postpartum Onset has its own set of complexities. In earlier *DSM*s, postpartum depression was an independent diagnosis. Now it is treated as a specifier. In part this recognizes that postpartum depressions are like any other depression, although whether there is a specific hormonal contribution is still debated. Three types of depression with postpartum onset can be distinguished. "Postpartum blues" are a common experience of women following the birth of a child. This is a mild form of depression that most likely results from the various stresses involved in having a child. Postpartum Onset depression is diagnosed when *DSM* criteria are met. These episodes are similar to other forms of depression and are likely to be the target of one form of treatment or another. Psychotic Depression with Postpartum Onset is the most severe form. Danger of harm to self and children is a concern in such cases, and although these incidents are rare, they often make the news. It is critical for these individuals to receive treatment. Michael O'Hara found

Clinical Vignette
A Case of Seasonal Pattern Depression

I once interviewed a woman who told me that for years she had developed an episode of depression each fall. She said she felt so depressed that she never felt like doing much and typically sat in her backyard daily and read. She was exposing herself to natural bright light and her episodes remitted in early spring. This year she said the depression was particularly severe, to the degree that she did not even feel like going out and reading. Instead she stayed in with the shades drawn. As a result, her depression did not remit in the spring, and she was finally seeking help for the depression. She had never heard of Seasonal Affective Disorder, which I described to her before referring her to a clinic where she could be evaluated and receive appropriate light therapy.

factors such as being single, having a lack of social support, and already having some symptoms of depression were predictors of Postpartum Onset depression (O'Hara, Rehm, & Campbell, 1982, 1983). *Other factors that have been identified as being associated with postpartum onset depression include tobacco use during the last 3 months of pregnancy, physical abuse before or during pregnancy, stress related to partner, trauma, or finances during pregnancy, and delivering a low-birth-weight infant* (Centers for Disease Control and Prevention, 2008).

Rapid Cycling (four or more bipolar episodes in a year) occurs in 10% to 20% of cases and is more frequent in women. In rare cases, Rapid Cycling may involve episodes that alternate within days or even hours. Rapid Cycling is associated with a poor prognosis. Poor prognosis in unipolar and bipolar mood disorders is associated with earlier onset, more severe episodes, and incomplete recovery from an initial episode.

Rapid Cycling is a term used to indicate four or more episodes per year

1.5   Differential Diagnosis

Within the mood diagnoses themselves, differential diagnosis can be a problem. A first episode of depression may be the prelude to later depression in its unipolar form, or it could be the first episode of a bipolar disorder. Likewise, a Manic Episode with irritable mood or a Mixed Episode may be difficult to differentiate from a MDE. In either case, inquiring into family history may help to make a determination. A lengthy period of depression (greater than 2 years) that does not remit may fit criteria for Dysthymia, but if it began with a full MDE then it is MDD in Partial Remission. Dysthymia can only be diagnosed in a person who has had MDD if it can be established that the person had Dysthymia first or if the MDD had fully remitted for at least a 2-month period before the Dysthymia began. If the Dysthymia occurs first and the person develops a MDE, then both Dysthymia and MDD diagnoses apply, a condition sometimes referred to as **Double Depression**. Dysthymia is distinguished from Adjustment Disorder with Depressed Mood by duration and by the fact that the latter is preceded by a clear stressor. Bereavement is not considered an instance of MDD unless it is persistent (greater than 2 months) or the person is functionally impaired. It should also be remembered that severity and duration criteria are important in differentiating MDD from normal periods of sadness.

DSM criteria require careful inquiry to differentiate episode types and patterns

Mood disorders may also be difficult to differentiate from anxiety disorders. In general, anxiety and depression are overlapping emotions and disorders of anxiety and mood have overlapping symptoms. The fact that the *DSM-IV* contains criteria for a diagnosis of Mixed Anxiety-Depressive Disorder in the appendix for possible disorders needing further study for inclusion in the *DSM* reflects this overlap. Both MDD and Generalized Anxiety Disorder (GAD) may involve excessive worrying. The criteria for GAD state that the diagnosis should not be made if the worry occurs only during an episode of depression. If the GAD occurs first, both diagnoses may apply. Individuals with MDD may be socially withdrawn, making differential diagnosis from Social Phobia or Avoidant Personality difficult. In this case, the clinician must

Mood and anxiety disorders overlap and mix together

establish that the social anxiety clearly preceded the MDD for both diagnoses to be given.

One of the symptoms of MDD is insomnia. Individuals who are having difficulty sleeping may present with only this symptom and be diagnosed erroneously with a Sleep Disorder. If insomnia is the presenting complaint is important to do a thorough evaluation for a mood disorder.

Psychotic forms of mood disorder may be difficult to separate from Schizophrenia

Mood disorders often appear in combination with psychotic symptoms, and this presents a number of differential diagnostic dilemmas. First, MDEs and Manic Episodes may occur With Psychotic Features. Typically these involve nonbizarre, mood-congruent delusions without hallucinations. The delusions occur only during the episode of mood disorder. If a person meets the primary criterion for Schizophrenia (Criterion A: two or more of delusions, hallucinations, disorganized speech, grossly disorganized or catatonic behavior or negative symptoms) and also meets criteria for a mood episode (MDE, Manic or Mixed), a diagnosis of Schizoaffective Disorder is made, either Depressive or Bipolar Type.

Substance use and medical disorders may cause depressions

The *DSM* has specific diagnoses for Substance-Induced Mood Disorder and Mood Disorder Due to a General Medical Condition. Substance use and various medical conditions often lead to depression. Substance-Induced Depressive Disorder may occur after prolonged use, during intoxication, or during withdrawal. In the case of a general medical condition, the medical diagnosis is recorded on Axis III. Dementia of the Alzheimer's Type often presents initially as depression in the elderly, masking the other symptoms of Alzheimer's disease. Making the diagnostic distinction requires careful evaluation. Depression may develop following the dementia, in which case both diagnoses may apply.

1.6   Comorbidities

Substance abuse and anxiety disorders are often codiagnosed with mood disorders

Depression can be comorbid with virtually any *DSM* diagnosis. It is quite common in alcohol and substance use disorders and with the anxiety disorders, prominently in Posttraumatic Stress Disorder and GAD. The distinction is often made between the primary and secondary of comorbid disorders, depending on which onset came first. Depression may be primary or secondary in its association with substance abuse. Use may lead to depression and depressed individuals may self-medicate with alcohol or other drugs. With the anxiety disorders, depression tends to be secondary. Clinical wisdom suggests that if the primary disorder is successfully treated, the secondary disorder may resolve as well. With substance-use disorders and depression, however, it is generally held that the substance disorder needs to be dealt with first because it may make treatment of the comorbid mood disorder difficult.

Depression may be comorbid with many medical disorders, typically as the secondary disorder. Comorbid depression is a negative prognostic consideration in the treatment of many medical disorders. A prominent example is seen in cardiovascular disorders; in these cases, approximately 20% of patients can be diagnosed with MDD and those with a diagnosis have more adverse outcomes (Thombs et al., 2008). Depression also is a risk factor for many medical disorders. Depressed individuals may be functionally impaired and exhibit poor self-healthcare. Depression as a comorbid disorder leads to higher healthcare costs.

1.7 Diagnostic Procedures and Documentation

There are a number of ways to assess depression. For the purposes of research, formal diagnoses are primarily determined via clinical interviews that can be semistructured or structured. Semistructured interviews are guided sets of questions and decision rules meant to be used by experts who may have to follow-up fairly open-ended questions with additional queries to decide whether a symptom is present or a diagnostic criterion is met. Structured interviews are intended to be employed by individuals with more limited training; for example, they are frequently used in epidemiological studies. These interviews tend to have more objective questions to which examinees give yes-or-no answers. Less clinical judgment and decision making is required of the interviewer.

Diagnosis is typically accomplished by interview; structured and semi-structured interviews have been developed for research purposes

In addition to the diagnostic interviews, there are also several instruments that are clinician rating scales. They assess one or more dimensions of depression as one or more continuous variables. They frequently involve rating symptoms on numerical scales. As with the semistructured interviews, clinical rating scales ordinarily assume that the rater is a clinical expert and clinical follow-up questions and judgment are often necessary.

Clinician rating scales are interview-based severity scales

Self-rating scales measure depression as a continuous variable rather than as a dichotomous variable. Scales vary in the degree to which they are proximal or distal to depression. Most forms of psychotherapy for depression focus on changing variables that are identified by some theory as central to depression. Measures of these variables may be considered proximal targets. It is assumed that changing the proximal targets will lead to changes in depression, and diminished depression in turn will have an influence on more distal measures such as general distress, adjustment, and life satisfaction. Examples of proximal measures would be scales developed to assess depressive cognitive distortions, negative attributional style, or pleasant activity levels. Proximal scales are often used in psychotherapy research to assess whether the target of an intervention has been modified by the specific intervention, e.g., have cognitive distortion scores been diminished by a cognitive therapy intervention?

Self-report scales give subjective reports of severity of depression

At the next more distal level are the measures of depression itself. Many scales of depression have been developed with variations in their approaches to sampling signs and symptoms of depression. These scales are often used to monitor progress in therapy for depression.

The most distal scales are subscales of larger inventories that measure psychopathology and distress more broadly. They typically include depression measures, but measure other forms of psychopathology as well. They are often used to assess whether the effects of an intervention for depression have generalized to other related symptoms of psychopathology.

In addition to these more traditional measures, there have been various attempts to assess depression by means of behavioral observations in various settings. These have been largely experimental, but they may come to play a larger role in depression assessment. The primary instruments in each of these domains will be reviewed briefly below.

Throughout this review, I will not offer a psychometric evaluation of the instruments. All of the scales have accumulated estimates of their reliability and validity in various settings with various samples. For the most part, these statistics are all good to excellent. Most of the scales were developed on the basis of logic rather than psychometrics; in fact, there is little basis for choice among the scales based on their psychometric properties. I will focus more on descriptions of the scales, their rationales, and potential uses. Those interested in the psychometric evaluation of scales should see Marsella, Hirshfeld, and Katz (1987), Nezu, Ronan, Meadows and McClure (2000), or Rehm (1988).

1.7.1   Diagnostic Interviews: Semistructured and Structured

Early developments in operational criteria for diagnoses were paralleled by developments in diagnostic interviews

In the 1960s it was recognized that the reliability of clinical diagnosis was a problem for researchers. Reliability of diagnosis both between and within research groups was low. One research group could not be sure that their sample was really comparable to another group's sample, and despite careful training within research groups, inter-rater reliability was often poor. The *Diagnostic and Statistical Manual* at the time (*DSM-II*) was of little help, only providing sometimes vague and general descriptions of disorders. The answer proposed was to develop clear, specific, and replicable criteria that could be more reliably applied in research. The first such proposal came from a group at Washington University in Saint Louis. What became known as the **Feighner Criteria**, after the first author (Feighner et al., 1972), were specific criteria for the major psychiatric disorders of concern to researchers. Soon after the Feighner criteria, another set of criteria was published for a wider set of disorders of interest. These became known as the **Research Diagnostic Criteria** (RDC) (Spitzer, Endicott, & Robins, 1975).The Spitzer group took the next step, which was to publish a standard set of questions to assess each of the RDC (Spitzer, Endicott, & Robins, 1978). This **Schedule for Affective Disorders and Schizophrenia** (SADS) became the first widely used semi-structured diagnostic interview in the US. It should be noted that there was a predecessor in the form of the Present State Examination (Wing, 1970). The PSE has standardized questions based on the International Classification of Diseases (ICD-8) and was intended to identify cases in epidemiological research. It is largely used in Europe and more for schizophrenia research than depression research.

Diagnostic Interviews: – Schedule for Affective Disorders and Schizophrenia (SADS) – Structured Clinical Interview for DSM (SCID) – Diagnostic Interview Schedule (DIS)

The SADS led the way as a semistructured interview for expert clinicians

The SADS came in three versions: the SADS regular form for making diagnoses based on the current episode; the SADS-L (for Lifetime) for making lifetime diagnoses; and the SADS-C (for Change) for assessing improvement or worsening of symptoms over a 1-week period. A version for use with children and their parents was also developed, the **Kiddie-SADS** (Chambers et al., 1985). The value of the RDC and the accompanying SADS in increasing reliability of diagnosis was recognized and they were readily accepted in the research world.

The SCID has become the standard for research diagnosis by expert clinicians

Spitzer became the chair of the *DSM-III* committee and incorporated the ideas of "operational criteria" from the Feighner and RDC tradition. He also continued the tradition of a parallel semistructured interview. The **Structured**

Clinical Interview for *DSM* (SCID) diagnosis first came out in a *DSM-III* version. It has subsequently been updated with each revision of the *DSM*. The SCID for the *DSM-IV* is published in several versions. First, there is a SCID-I for Axis-I disorders (First, Spitzer, Gibbon, & Williams, 1995) and a SCID-II for Axis-II disorders (First, Spitzer, Girgus, & Williams, 1997b). Second, the SCID-I comes in research (SCID-I RV) and clinical versions (SCID-I CV). The research version is more detailed in that it covers criteria for specifiers and a longer list of diagnoses, and it is more easily modifiable for special-purpose research projects. The research version includes patient, nonpatient, and a second patient version with a brief psychotic screen (for patient populations in which psychosis is rare). The research version is published by the Biometrics Research Department of Columbia University and the clinical version (First, Spitzer, Girgus, & Williams, 1997a) is published by the American Psychiatric Association. The clinical version is constructed differently with a reuseable administration booklet and single-use response sheets. Both are constructed in modules for different sets of diagnoses, and both involve sequences of questions with decision points, e.g., if neither criterion A nor B is met, skip to the next diagnosis. The mood disorder module covers all of the diagnoses described in the first chapter. Its purpose is fulfilled in that reliabilities for the SCID modules are generally good.

Although the SCID has become the primary diagnostic instrument for research and clinical purposes, it has its drawbacks. Despite the "skip to" instructions, it can be quite lengthy. With patients with multiple diagnoses or those who cannot express themselves clearly, the full interview can go for 2 hours or longer. Its length makes it particularly cumbersome for epidemiological research. For these purposes another instrument was constructed by the National Institute of Mental Health, the **Diagnostic Interview Schedule** (DIS) (Robins, Helzer, Croughan, & Ratcliff, 1981). The DIS differs from the SCID in that it was designed for lay interviewers with specific training. Questions are written to elicit yes-or-no answers, thus minimizing any clinical judgment on the part of the interviewer. The format is also easier in that there are no "skip to" instructions. Data can be computer scored. Different diagnostic criteria can be employed and the DIS has been scored for Feighner, RDC, and *DSM-III*, *DSM-IIIR*, and *DSM-IV* criteria (Eaton et al., 1997). Use of the DIS has been fairly limited to large-scale epidemiological studies, but a child version has become much more popular because of the use of the simpler format with children (Shaffer et al., 1996).

> The DIS was created for epidemiological research with trained but nonexpert interviewers

1.7.2   Clinician Rating Scales

1.7.2.1   Hamilton Depression Rating Scale

The best known of the instruments designed for a clinician to rate the severity of depression is the Hamilton Depression Rating Scale (Hamilton, 1960, 1967). The scale was rationally derived. Hamilton originally intended the scale to be used to assess severity of depression in already-diagnosed patients. He also recommended that two raters fill it out and the sum of their scores be used as the reported score. This recommendation has not been followed by most users. The original scale consisted of 21 items, although only 17 were meant to

> Clinician Rating Scales:
> – Hamilton
> – Montgomery-Asberg
> – Raskin 3-Item

> The Hamilton was devised as a measure of severity in already diagnosed patients

be scored. Each item is rated on either a 3- or 5-point scale. Minor variations in the scale were made between the 1960 and 1967 versions. The scale continues to be used in different versions ranging from the 17-item form to a 24-item form to which several cognitive symptom items have been added. The scale has also been embedded in or extracted from interview protocols. A subset of items has been used as an "endogenomorphic" subscale to assess the degree of endogenous depression.

The Hamilton is heavily weighted with somatic items (eight), which is perhaps appropriate given its frequent use in assessing depression in drug trials. There are five items assessing behavioral complaints, two cognitive items and two affect items in the original 17. All of the nine *DSM* criterion items are covered. There is no manual for the instrument and no normative information or cutoff scores are provided in the original reports. Different researchers use either a cut-off of under 10 or a cut-off of under 7 to define who is normal or no longer depressed. Scores above 25 are considered severe and are typical of inpatient samples. Outpatients typically score in the upper teens to lower twenties on average. Interrater reliabilities reported by a number of sources have generally been excellent with the exceptions of a couple of items. Item total correlations range from 0.22 to 0.67 (Rehm & O'Hara, 1985). Concurrent validity with other scales has been reported to be high by a number of authors. The Hamilton is also sensitive to change as demonstrated in multiple studies.

In sum, despite a rather psychometrically unsophisticated beginning, the Hamilton has accumulated data suggesting that it has acceptable reliability and validity. The Hamilton has become the most widely used clinician rating scale in the depression literature. One drawback is the fact that it is used in so many variations. Due to its wide usage, however, it is likely to continue to be used for comparability to earlier studies until a more sophisticated instrument is constructed.

1.7.2.2   Montgomery-Asberg Depression Rating Scale

The Montgomery-Asberg was developed specifically for assessing outcome in research trials

The Montgomery-Asberg was developed for the specific purpose of assessing change in clinical trials (Montgomery & Asberg, 1979). The scale consists of 10 items selected from a larger 65-item rating scale on the basis of their sensitivity to change and their item-total correlations. Each item is rated on a 7-point scale, from 0 for absent to 6 for severe. Anchor points involve increasing intensity and frequency of symptoms. Psychometric data are limited. The scale has been used more in Europe than in the United States.

1.7.2.3   Raskin Three Area Rating Scale

The Raskin is a quick estimate of depression severity

This scale was designed as a rapid method for selecting subjects for research (Raskin, Schulterbrandt, Reatig, & McKeon, 1969; Raskin, Schulterbrandt, Reatig, & Rice, 1967). Three areas, Verbal Report, Behavior, and Secondary Symptoms of Depression, are rated on 5-point scales from "not at all" to "very much." The sum of the three ratings yields a score from 3 to 15. The scale is now commonly used as a quick adjunct clinical rating of improvement in clinical trials. Reliability and validity data are somewhat scarce, but the scale has gained fairly wide use.

1.7.3   Scales Measuring Constructs Related to Depression

Several types of rating scales are useful in assessing depression (Table 4). Many scales assess depression-related phenomena such as hopelessness or suicide tendency. Consistent with the treatment theme of the book, I will focus on scales relevant to assessing depression in clinical and research settings in which depression is being treated. The first group of scales was designed to assess target constructs. For the most part, they were developed with the idea of assessing constructs that theories of depression have identified as central to the development of depression. Modifying these constructs is theoretically the mechanism by which depression is reduced in treatment.

A number of scales measure constructs that are theoretically the basis of depression

Table 4
Measures of Depression-Related Constructs

Pleasant Events Scale

Unpleasant Events Scale

Problem-Solving Inventory

Social Adjustment Scale

Attributional Style Questionnaire

Automatic Thoughts Questionnaire–R

Dysfunctional Attitudes Scale

Self-Control Questionnaire for Depression

Frequency of Self-Reinforcement Questionnaire

Self-Control Schedule/Learned Resourcefulness Inventory Scale

1.7.3.1   Pleasant Events Schedule and Unpleasant Events Schedule

The Pleasant Events Schedule (PES) and Unpleasant Events Schedule (UES) are scales developed to assess the amount of reinforcing and punishing behavior that a person is experiencing in his or her day-to-day life. The assumption is that therapy for depression should increase PES scores and decrease UES scores. Peter Lewinsohn and his colleagues developed the PES (MacPhillamy & Lewinsohn, 1971, 1972, 1976, 1982) and the UES (Lewinsohn & Talkington, 1979) as part of Lewinsohn's clinical research program developing behavioral interventions for depression (Lewinsohn, Biglan, & Zeiss, 1976). The PES is intended to assess the amount of reinforcement a person receives. It consists of 320 potentially enjoyable events and is used in two ways. As a retrospective instrument, individuals rate each event that has occurred in the last 30 days. Ratings are on a 3-point scale for frequency (0 = not happened; 1 = happened a few times; and 2 = happened often) and for how enjoyable or potentially enjoyable it was or would be, on a second 3-point scale (0 = not pleasant; 1 = somewhat pleasant; and 2 = very pleasant). Three scores can be derived: Activity Level is the sum of the first ratings; Reinforcement Potential is the sum of the second rating; and Obtained Reinforcement is the sum of the cross products. In

The PES measures reinforcing behavior according to Lewinsohn's behavioral model

its second form, shorter lists of items are selected for a specific individual and serve as daily checklists of events. Validity data include the fact that all three scores on the 30-day format differentiate between depressed and not-depressed persons. As daily activity checklists, the PES correlates with daily fluctuations in mood (Lewinsohn & Graf, 1973; Lewinsohn & Libet, 1972).

The UES is used and scored in a parallel manner. It also differentiates between depressed and nondepressed samples and correlates with depression scores. As a daily check list it is negatively correlated with mood and with the PES. The UES adds variance in predicting mood fluctuations over the PES alone (Lewinsohn & Talkington, 1979). An Interpersonal Events Schedule (Youngren & Lewinsohn, 1980) has also been published. This 160-item schedule was developed because interpersonal events are held to be particularly important in their relationship to depression. Ten different interpersonal events are assessed.

1.7.3.2   Problem-Solving Inventory

Problem-solving deficiency can be seen as a basis for depression

The Problem-Solving Inventory (PSI) (Heppner & Petersen, 1982) was developed to assess individuals' perceptions of their responses to personal problems. Respondents indicate on a 6-point Likert scale the degree to which they agree with each of 35 statements (from 1 = strongly agree to 6 = strongly disagree). In addition to a total score, three subscale scores can be derived for Problem-Solving Confidence, Approach-Avoidance Style, and Personal Control. Problem-solving is a social skill that has been found to be deficient in depressed individuals (Nezu & Ronan, 1985, 1988) and it is a potential target for therapy.

1.7.3.3   Social Adjustment Scale

Poor social adjustment is central to IPT, but it is also an important consideration in many forms of treatment

The Social Adjustment Scale (SAS) represents another approach to assessing social skills that are relevant to depression. Interpersonal Therapy (Klerman, Weissman, Rounceville, & Chevron, 1984) is a particular form of therapy derived from a Sullivanian psychodynamic perspective that holds that depression is caused by disruptions in interpersonal relationships. The nature of the therapy is to identify the disruption and to repair it. The developers of the therapy felt that there was no appropriate scale to measure these disruptions and created the SAS to fill this need (Paykel, Weissman, Prusoff, & Tonks, 1971). The SAS is a 48-item semistructured interview that allows a trained examiner to rate each item on 5-point scales specific to the item. Scores are averaged for subscales relating to five social roles: Work; Social and Leisure Activities; Relations with Extended Family; Intimate Relations; and Parenthood. The SAS can also be scored on six factor-analytically derived subscales: Work Performance; Interpersonal Friction; Inhibited Communication; Submissive Dependency; Family Attachment; and Anxious Rumination. High scores indicate poorer social adjustment. Although specifically relevant to Interpersonal Therapy, assessing social adjustment is relevant to the outcome of virtually any form of therapy for depression as a distal measure.

1.7.3.4   Attributional Style Questionnaire

Attributional Style is central to helplessness theory

The Attributional Style Questionnaire (ASQ) (Petersen, et al., 1982; Seligman, Abramson, Semmel, & von Bayer, 1979) was developed to assess constructs derived from the attributional formulation of Seligman's learned helplessness theory of depression (Abramson, Seligman, & Teasdale, 1978). The theory assumes that a psychological vulnerability to depression is based on the way in which individuals make inferences about the causes of positive and negative events that occur in their lives. Individuals who have a tendency to assume that they are personally responsible for the negative events in their lives and that these events result from their personal general and enduring characteristics are more likely to become depressed when a major negative life event occurs. These depression-prone individuals are also likely to attribute positive events to external causes that are specific and fleeting. The ASQ assesses the tendency to make internal, stable, general attributions to negative events and external, unstable, specific attributions to positive events, a depressive attributional style. The scale consists of six positive and six negative hypothetical events that are related to either achievement or affiliation. Respondents are required to write down what they think the cause of the event would be if it occurred to them. Next they rate the causes on 7-point Likert scales for internality, stability, and generality. Last, they rate the hypothetical importance of the event. Thus, four ratings are obtained for each of the 12 events. Scores can be derived for positive events, negative events, achievement events, affiliative events, or combinations thereof. The scale is somewhat cumbersome for clinical use and has largely been used in research on learned helplessness. Changing attributional style is a component of various interventions for depression.

1.7.3.5 Automatic Thoughts Questionnaire–Revised

The Automatic Thoughts Questionnaire–Revised (ATQ-R) was devised to assess negative and positive self-statements (Kendall, Howard, & Hays, 1989). A predominance of negative thoughts about oneself is held to be a vulnerability factor for depression by cognitive theorists. The ATQ-R consists of 40 self-referent statements that are each rated on a 5-point scale for the frequency with which they are estimated to have occurred in the last week (from 0 = not at all to 4 = all the time). The original scale consisted on 30 negative statements and the revised form added 10 positive statements. In theory, nondepressed individuals will have at least as many positive as negative thoughts about themselves and depressed individuals will have a preponderance of negative thoughts. Although it was originally conceived as a vulnerability measure, the ATQ-R is probably more of a symptom measure, but could be very useful as an index of changes in negative thinking over time or in therapy, especially a cognitively oriented therapy.

> The ATQ-R is an attempt to assess negative thinking along the lines of Beck's cognitive model

1.7.3.6 Dysfunctional Attitudes Scale

Somewhat similar to the ATQ-R, the Dysfunctional Attitudes Scale (DAS) was developed to assess maladaptive negative thoughts and assumptions (Weissman & Beck, 1978). Beck's cognitive theory of depression hypothesizes that depressed people have a negative view of themselves, the world, and the future. This scale was designed to assess these negative cognitions. The original scale consisted of 100 items, but it is now available in two 40-item alternative forms. Each item is rated on a 7-point Likert Scale (1 = totally agree; 7 = totally disagree). The original intent was to assess the silent assumptions that make a person vulnerable to depression, but this scale is also a symptom

> The DAS measures negative thinking

scale assessing the negativity of thinking by depressed individuals. The scale differentiates between depressed and nondepressed individuals.

1.7.3.7   Self-Control Questionnaire for Depression

The original Concepts Test was devised by Carolyn Fuchs (Fuchs & Rehm, 1977). It was intended to assess the attitudes, beliefs, and behaviors that characterized depressive self-control skills as hypothesized by the self-control model of depression (Rehm, 1977). The scale was revised and expanded a number of times with a major revision in 2003 (Anderson, Rehm, & Mehta, 2003). The Self-Control Questionnaire for Depression (SCQD) was revised from an expanded item pool and was intended to assess seven hypothesized deficits in self-control that make a person vulnerable to depression and/or which are self-control symptoms of depression. Factor analyses and structural equation modeling led to a final nine subscales under a three-factor higher-order model. The subscales follow: Under the factor Negative Monitoring: (1) monitoring control of mood; (2) attributions for negative events; (3) internal standards; (4) self-punishment regarding effort; and (5) self-punishment regarding self; under the factor Goal Orientation, (6) future orientation; (7) attributions for positive events; and (8) goal setting; and under the factor Self-Reinforcement, (9) self-reinforcement. The scale is intended for use in conjunction with the Self-Management Therapy Program for depression (Rehm & Adams, 2009). The therapy program targets a series of constructs and the scale is intended to measure each of these targeted constructs. Various versions of the questionnaire were found to correlate with measures of depression and to change with improvement in therapy.

1.7.3.8   Frequency of Self-Reinforcement Questionnaire

The Frequency of Self-Reinforcement Questionnaire (FSRQ) (Heiby, 1983) was developed to assess attitudes and beliefs relevant to the self-control model of depression (Rehm, 1977). The questionnaire consist of 30 items, of which 15 represent positive attitudes toward self-reinforcement and 15 represent negative depressive attitudes. Each statement is answered as true or false as it applies to the respondent. Each nondepressed answer is scored 1 and each depressed answer is scored 0, thus higher scores (maximum 30) reflect a more positive, nondepressed attitude. The questionnaire has been validated by correlating it with self-praise in experimental tasks. It also correlates with measures of depression. The scale has been used in a variety of research endeavors, especially with college students.

1.7.3.9   Self-Control Schedule/Learned Resourcefulness Scale

When this instrument was originally published as the Self-Control Schedule (SCS) (Rosenbaum, 1980), Rosenbaum noted that high self-control equated to learned resourcefulness, a concept opposite to learned helplessness. He thus renamed the scale the Learned Resourcefulness Scale (LRS) and connected it to Seligman's learned helplessness theory (Rosenbaum & Jaffe, 1983). The original conception viewed self-control quite broadly and the emphasis on the positive resourcefulness side of the construct gives the scale broad potential. The scale is made up of 36 items designed to reflect skills in coping with problems. Items are rated on a 6-point Likert scale (from –3 for "very uncharacteristic of me," to +3 for "very characteristic of me"). Ten items are reverse scored and the possible range of scores is –108 to +108. Several studies have found that the scale is a general predictor of positive outcome in psychotherapy for depression, i.e., better initial coping skills predicts better response to psychotherapy (Rude & Rehm, 1991). This is a useful scale that is associated with multiple theoretical approaches.

1.7.4 Depression Scales

Numerous depression scales have evolved since the 1960s (Table 5).

Table 5
Depression Scales

Beck Depression Inventory-II

Carroll Depression Scale-R

Diagnostic Inventory for Depression

Zung Self-Rating Depression Scale

Center for Epidemiological Studies Depression Scale

Positive Affect/Negative Affect Scale

1.7.4.1 Beck Depression Inventory

Although it was originally published as a clinician rating scale, the Beck Depression Inventory (BDI) is used currently as a self-report scale. The original version was published in 1961 (Beck, Ward, Mendelsohn, Mock, & Erbaugh, 1961) and a revised version, the BDI-II came out in 1996 (Beck, Steer, & Brown, 1996). The inventory consists of 21 multiple-choice items, each representing variations in level of a particular symptom of depression. Nineteen of the items are scored 0 to 3 for ascending levels of severity. The other two items are symptoms that can deviate from normal either by increasing or decreasing. Depressed persons may lose their appetite or they may overeat, and they may have insomnia or may sleep excessively. Increasing severity in either direction is scored on the same 4-point scale. The content of the BDI is weighted somewhat toward cognitive items in line with Beck's cognitive conception of depression, but the items do cover all of the *DSM* symptoms.

The BDI has become the most widely used self-report instrument for assessing depression severity

The BDI, in both its forms, is the most widely used depression self-report measure for both research and clinical uses. Its psychometrics have been extensively studied and reviews are available (Beck, Steer, & Garbin, 1988; Dozois, Dobson, & Ahnberg, 1998). The BDI-II manual suggests the following guidelines for interpretation of scores: 0–13 minimum depression; 14–19 mild depression; 20–28 moderate depression; and 29–63 severe depression.

1.7.4.2 Carroll Depression Scales–Revised (CDS-R)

The rationale for the original Carroll Depression Scales (CDS) was to create a self-report scale parallel to the clinician-rated 17-item Hamilton Depression

The CDS-R was devised as a self-report parallel of the Hamilton

Rating Scale (Carroll, Feinberg, Smouse, Rawson, & Greden, 1981). Hamilton items are rated on either 5- or 3-point scales. The CDS is made up of items representing each rating point to which the respondent answers "yes" or "no." The original scale had 52 items corresponding to the maximum score of 52 on the Hamilton. It is assumed that endorsers of higher ratings on the Hamilton will also endorse the lower-rated alternatives. The revised scale (CDS-R) is made up of 61 items and was designed to be compatible also with *DSM-IV* (Carroll, 1998). Items are scored either 0–1 or 1–0 with a range of 0 to 61. Item order is scrambled so that the related Hamilton ratings are not consecutive. The parallel structure with the Hamilton Depression Rating Scale is a positive feature of this scale, although it has not been widely adopted beyond some medication trials.

1.7.4.3   Diagnostic Inventory for Depression

The DID is a self-report instrument that yields a diagnosis as well as a severity index

An original scale, the Inventory to Diagnose Depression, was developed as a self-report instrument that permitted at least a provisional diagnosis of Major Depressive Disorder according to *DSM-III* criteria (Zimmerman, Coryell, Corenthal, & Wilson, 1986). An updated version, named the Diagnostic Inventory for Depression (DID) (Zimmerman, Sheeran, & Young, 2004) was developed to make this instrument consistent with *DSM-IV* criteria. The revision eliminated the hopelessness and irritability equivalents for dysphoric mood and added the social impairment criteria consistent with the changes from *DSM-III* to *DSM-IV*. The inventory consists of 38 items. Nineteen items assess symptom severity as defined by the *DSM* criteria. Other items assess psychosocial functioning and quality of life and subscale scores can be obtained. Items are rated on 5-point Likert scales from 0 to 4. For the purposes of diagnosis, items can be scored as symptom present or absent. For loss-of-interest and pleasure items, a score of 3 or more indicates symptom present, for all other items a score of 2 or more indicates symptom present. The scale yields a dichotomous indication of whether or not diagnostic criteria are met, and it provides a severity score. The ability to make a diagnosis, even though it must be considered tentative because it is not made by the judgment of an expert clinician, is a great advantage for many types of research. Even in studies where severity is the primary experimental variable of interest, it can be of considerable value to have an estimate of the prevalence of the diagnosis in the sample. The DID has a wide range of potential uses in research and in clinical screening contexts.

1.7.4.4   Zung Self-Rating Depression Scale

The Zung is a self-report instrument frequently used in medication trials

The Zung Self-Rating Depression Scale (SDS) was devised to assess three factors commonly found in factor analyses of depression scales: pervasive affect, physiological concomitants, and psychological concomitants (Zung, 1965, 1974). The scale consists of 20 items, 10 of which are written in a positive direction and 10 in a negative direction. Respondents rate each item on a 4-point frequency scale (1 = a little; 2 = some; 3 = a good part; and 4 = most of the time). Scores are expressed in a percentage index. The total score is divided by 80, the maximum score, and then multiplied by 100. Zung suggests cutoffs as follows: below 50 = normal range; 50–59 = minimal to mild depression; 60–69 moderate depression; and 70–99 severe depression. Because of its brevity, the Zung SDS is useful for clinical screening and it is an easy addition to many research protocols. The Zung has been extensively used in medication trials.

1.7.4.5   Center for Epidemiological Studies Depression Scale

As its name implies, the Center for Epidemiological Studies Depression Scale (CES-D) was developed under the auspices of the Center for Epidemiological Studies of the National Institutes of Mental Health (Radloff, 1977). It was developed to be used in epidemiological studies, and thus it assesses depression in the normal range and above. Most of the scales reviewed here were developed to assess severity of depression in patient populations. When these scales are used with normal populations, their distributions are highly skewed, with most people scoring in the low range and fewer people scoring in the higher ranges. The CES-D is designed to assess symptoms of depression in a variety of populations, including psychiatric, medical, and the general population. The scale consists of 20 first-person statements regarding a depressive symptom. Respondents indicate on a 4-point scale the frequency with which they have felt this way during the past week: 0 = rarely or none of the time (less than one day); 1 = some of the time (1–2 days); 2 = occasionally or a moderate amount of the time (3–4 days); and 3 = most or all of the time (5–7 days). Sixteen items are scored in a negative direction and four in a positive direction. Content of the scale was designed to sample depressed mood, feelings of guilt and worthlessness, feelings of helplessness and hopelessness, psychomotor retardation, loss of appetite, and sleep disturbance. Given the nature of its development, the CES-D is a good choice for assessing symptoms of depression in normal populations, such as in research with undergraduates.

The CES-D was devised for epidemiological research and has a normal distribution in a normal population

1.7.4.6   Positive Affect Negative Affect Scale

Rather than a measure of the construct of clinical depression, the Positive Affect Negative Affect Scale (PANAS) (Watson, Clark, & Tellegen, 1988) is a measure of the basic emotions defining depression. As discussed earlier, research on basic emotion tends to categorize emotions such as anxiety and depression into two or three dimensions (Clark & Watson, 1991). One such solution defines depression as high negative affect and low positive affect. The PANAS consists of two scales: positive affect, and negative affect. Each scale has 10 items consisting of an adjective that is rated from 1 (very slightly or not at all) to 5 (extremely). The scale has been used with a variety of time frames, including "at the present moment," "today," "the past few days," "the past week," and "how you feel on the average." Thus, this is a relatively short instrument that can be used to assess momentary state to recent mood to average state. It will probably be used primarily as a research instrument.

The PANAS measures basic positive and negative dimensions of emotion

1.7.5   Inventories with Depression Scales

A number of inventories that are intended to measure general psychopathology include depression scales (Table 6). They are useful when depression is

Table 6
Inventories with Depression Scales

Minnesota Multiphasic Personality Inventory–2 (MMPI-2)

Depression, Anxiety and Stress Scales

Symptom Checklist-90-R

Brief Psychiatric Rating Scale

Millon Clinical Multiaxial Inventory

only part of a broader assessment of emotional state and when general distress along with depression are to be assessed.

1.7.5.1   Minnesota Multiphasic Personality Inventory–2 (MMPI-2)

The MMPI-2 is the most commonly used personality scale in the United States, and it includes a depression scale

The most widely used psychological inventory in the United States is the Minnesota Multiphasic Personality Inventory (MMPI) (Hathaway & McKinley, 1951), which was published in a revised and restandardized form as the MMPI-2 in 1989 (Butcher, Dahlstrom, Graham, Tellegen, & Kraemmer, 1989). The MMPI-2 consists of 567 items in a true–false response format. It takes 1 to 2 hours to complete. The inventory is made up of three validity scales and ten clinical scales. The MMPI has also been used as an item bank for creating many other scales. The Depression Scale (D) is scale 2 of the clinical scales. It consists of 57 items that were empirically selected because they were responded to differentially by a psychiatric sample with various forms of depression. As with all of the scales, scores are expressed as T-scores (mean 50 and standard deviation 10). Elevations on the scales above 65 are considered clinically significant.

As a stand-alone scale, the D scale takes about 12 minutes to complete and is a measure of severity of depression. There is also a shorter 30-item scale derived from the MMPI termed the D-30 (Dempsey, 1964). In outcome research on the treatment of depression, the total MMPI-2 is sometimes used as an index of generalization of treatment effect by looking at total elevations of the scales. In clinical use, however, the value of the MMPI-2 is in profile interpretation. Combinations of the two to four most elevated scales have been studied and various "atlases" have been published to interpret them based on the belief that the profile tells a more detailed story than the individual scales. For example, a 1–2 or 2–1 profile (highest elevations on scales 1, Hypochondriasis, and 2, Depression) would be indicative of a person whose depression is expressed with an emphasis on somatic complaints, whereas a 2–6 or 6–2 profile (highest elevations on scales on scales 6, Paranoia, and 2, Depression) would be indicative of an angry, hostile depressed person who is suspicious and blaming of others. Many profile types with extensive interpretive information in different patient populations have been described. Various services are available to provide computerized interpretations of profiles. Thus, the main advantage of the MMPI-2 for both clinical and research purposes is in looking at differences in profiles in depressed samples. Subtypes may respond differently to different treatments.

1.7.5.2   Depression, Anxiety and Stress Scales

Although not a full personality inventory like the MMPI, the Depression, Anxiety and Stress Scales (DASS) consists of three scales measuring depression, anxiety, and stress. Each scale has 14 items for a total of 42. Each item is scored on a 4-point scale from 0 = did not apply to me at all, to 3 = applied to me very much or most of the time. The scale is useful as a relatively brief depression measure if anxiety and stress are also of interest, as in certain research contexts. It may be especially useful for differentiating depressed mood and anxiety.

The DASS is a research scale for assessing the related emotions of depression and anxiet

1.7.5.3   Symptom Checklist-90–Revised (SCL-90-R)

The Symptom Checklist-90–Revised (SCL-90-R) is a list of 90 symptoms that provides scores on nine clinical dimensions: anxiety, depression, hostility, interpersonal sensitivity, obsessive–compulsive, paranoid ideation, phobic anxiety, psychoticism, and somatization. Responses are made on a 5-point scale from 0 = not at all to 4 = extremely. The depression scale consists of 13 items representing a range of depressive symptoms. It is a useful scale if symptom dimensions rather than diagnostic differences are of interest. It is also often used as a general psychopathology measure using a total score.

The SCL-90-R is often used as a general measure of psychopathology and has a depression scale

1.7.5.4   Brief Psychiatric Rating Scale

The Brief Psychiatric Rating Scale (BPRS) was devised as a rapid clinician rating scale for evaluating change in clinical trials. The original scale (Overall & Gorman, 1962) consisted of 16 symptom items that yielded four syndrome subscale scores. An expanded version (Lukoff, Liberman, & Nuechterlein, 1986) contains 24 items that are grouped into five subscales: thought disorder, withdrawal, anxiety–depression, hostility–suspicion, and activity. Each item is rated on a 7-point scale from 1 = absent to 7 = extremely severe. The BPRS has achieved popularity as a measure of clinical symptom dimensions in clinical trials of medications in both the depression and schizophrenia research literatures. Given its brevity, it is useful for clinical settings as well. As a measure of severe pathology, it is likely to be used most frequently in inpatient or residential settings.

The BPRS is intended as a quick scale for the use of a clinician

1.7.5.5   Millon Clinical Multiaxial Inventory (MCMI)

The latest version of the Millon is the Millon Clinical Multiaxial Inventory-III (MCMI-III). This inventory is intended to measure *DSM* Axis-II psychopathology and major Axis-I syndromes in a relatively short format. It consists of 175 true–false items that yield 11 Clinical Personality Pattern scales, reflecting essentially personality disorder symptoms: three Severe Personality Pathology scales, assessing Schizotypal, Borderline, and Paranoid symptoms; seven Clinical Syndrome scales, which include two related to depression, Bipolar Manic and Dysthymic; three Severe Clinical Syndrome scales, Thought Disorder, Major Depression, and Delusional Disorder; and three Modifying Indices scales assessing test-taking attitudes. From the perspective of assessment of mood disorder pathology, the MCMI-III has three relevant scales, Bipolar Manic, Dysthymia, and Major Depression, thus giving a broader perspective than most inventories, which have a single depression index. The primary strength of the MCMI-III is in assessing personality disorders, which

The Millon focuses on personality disorders, but includes three scales related to depression

it does in a manner consistent with the *DSM*, but also derived from a coherent theoretical framework for understanding personality disorders (Millon & Davis, 1996). It would be most useful in research or clinical work where personality pathology is of interest along with depression.

Other scales and inventories exist that may be useful in assessing depression as a trait and as a state, but those reviewed above are the primary and most commonly used assessments. They vary in their approaches and choosing among them depends on the clinician's or researcher's needs in a particular context.

1.7.6   Behavioral Measures

Behavioral measures are largely limited to research uses with a variety of methods

A number of researchers have explored approaches to the direct measure of depressed behavior. Peter Lewinsohn's clinical research program using behavior therapy for depression required methods for coding verbal behavior in interview and therapy contexts to be devised. Slowed or retarded speech was recorded by an observer who used a hand counter to count the number of words spoken in 30-second intervals by a chronically depressed psychiatric patient (Robinson & Lewinsohn, 1973). Speech rate appeared to be a stable depression characteristic that was modifiable using reinforcement techniques.

Lewinsohn and his colleagues (Lewinsohn, Weinstein, & Alper, 1970) followed a different line of reasoning in studies of verbal behavior in group therapy for depression. Based on the idea that depression involves deficits in social skill, they coded the verbal behavior of mildly depressed volunteers in 18 sessions of group therapy. Two observers kept track of four indices of social skill: (1) total amount of behavior emitted by and directed toward an individual; (2) use of positive and negative reactions by each individual; (3) interpersonal efficiency ratio, i.e., the number of verbal behaviors directed toward an individual relative to the number emitted by that individual; (4) range of interactions with others. It is assumed that greater social skill would be indicated by more speech activity, greater use of positive reactions, a high ratio of received to emitted behavior, and interacting with a higher number of members of the group. Feedback on these measures and their interpretation was given to group members at the beginning of each session and the feedback became the primary topic of discussion and the impetus for efforts by individuals to improve their scores. Lewinsohn's research group has used this general concept of measuring interactive behavior and using it as feedback and as a means of identifying targets for change in family and marital therapy (Hops et al., 1987; Lewinsohn & Shaffer, 1971; Lewinsohn & Shaw, 1969).

My research group at the University of Pittsburgh, and later at the University of Houston, explored coding of verbal and nonverbal behavior in the context of evaluating the outcome of a cognitive-behavioral group therapy for depression, the Self-Management Therapy program. Fuchs and Rehm (Fuchs & Rehm, 1977) videotaped 10-minute segments of therapist-absent interaction among group members during the first and last therapy sessions. The number of statements by each individual was counted as a simple assessment of verbal activity level. Verbal activity increased more among the experimental than control subjects from first to last session. In our next study (Rehm, Fuchs, Roth, Kornblith, & Romano, 1979), we coded nine verbal and nonverbal behaviors in similar first- and last-session interactions. Last-session scores, with first-session scores covaried, differed significantly between conditions for negative self-statements, negative references to others, and overall depression ratings. Of 11 coded behaviors from pre- and post-therapy interviews in another study (Rehm et al., 1981), only loudness and latency of responding demonstrated therapy effects.

Coding verbal behavior of married couples has been part of a number of studies, some of which included interventions. McLean, Ogston, and Grauer (1973) describe a simplified version of Lewinsohn's coding scheme in a study of eclectic behavior therapy for depressed individuals and their spouses. Participants and their spouses made 30-minute recordings of problem discussions in their homes. The tapes were scored for positive and negative initiations and reactions by each spouse. After therapy, couples decreased in negative actions and reactions in contrast to control couples. In a German study by Hautzinger, Linden, and Hoffman (1982), distressed couples with and without a depressed spouse taped eight conversations of up to 45 minutes on eight different topics. From these tapes, codes for 28 verbal behaviors were extracted. Couples with a depressed spouse showed more uneven, negative, and asymmetrical verbal interactions with frequent focus on somatic and psychological complaints by the depressed spouse. The authors concluded that depressive complaints represent a pattern of short-term coercive control by the depressed spouse, but long-term dissatisfaction in both spouses. Hinchliffe, Hooper, and Roberts (1978) coded the interactions of depressed inpatients with their spouses and with an opposite-sex stranger during and after hospitalization. A control group of surgical patients and their spouses was also included. The interactions of the depressed patients were generally characterized by greater tension and expressions of negativity. There were higher levels of disruption, negative emotional outbursts, and incongruity between channels of communication. Interactions with spouses were more pathological than those with strangers. After hospitalization, the interactions of male depressed patients with their wives resembled those of surgical patient couples; however, interactions of depressed women patients showed little change from the time when they were hospitalized.

A study by Jacobson and Anderson (1982) looked at the timing of verbal interactions between depressed and nondepressed participants in their interactions with a confederate. Depressed participants made more negative self-statements and, when conditional timing was examined, depressed participants were more likely to self-disclose when confederate remarks did not directly solicit self-disclosure. This tendency is seen as a primary reason nondepressed people respond negatively to depressed individuals in social interactions (Coyne, 1976).

Overt motor behavior has been coded in a number of other studies. Differences between depressed and nondepressed individuals have been reported on a number of observable dimensions. For example, Waxer (1976) observed depressed participants to show posture differences, and Ekman and Friesen (1974) found differences in gestures and facial expressions in mouth and eye muscles. Williams, Barlow, and Agras (1972) described a time-sampling procedure with 10 depressed psychiatric inpatients whereby at some random point in each 30-minute interval, a trained observer recorded the presence or absence of each of four response classes: (1) talking; (2) smiling; (3) motor activity (further defined by 10 specific activities); and (4) time out of room. Scores were used as an index of behavioral severity of depression. The behavioral index correlated with Beck Depression Inventory and Hamilton depression ratings, and was more predictive than either of these scales of post-hospital improvement.

A technically sophisticated methodology for recording overt motor movement of psychiatric patients has been described by Kupfer and colleagues (Kupfer, Detre, Foster, Tucker, & Delgado, 1972). A miniature transmitter containing a magnetic ball in an inductance coil is encased in a small cylinder worn on a wrist band. Receivers in the ceiling of the psychiatric unit read out data continuously as number of counts per minute as the ball rolls back and forth in the coil. This group reported good reliability between receivers on different wrists and wrists versus ankle placements. Depressed unipolar patients were found to be more active than depressed bipolar patients. Recording 24 hours per day allowed for comparisons and close correspondence with sleep measures as well (Kupfer & Foster, 1972; Kupfer, Foster, Reich, Thompson, & Weiss, 1976). A student and I (O'Hara & Rehm, 1985) did a similar study of overt motor activity and depression using simple mechanical pedometers, but found no correlation between activity and daily mood.

A number of researchers have experimented with assessing the verbal or overt motor behavior of depressed people. Findings have elucidated some aspects of the interpersonal interactions of people, but none of the methodologies has developed into a standard form of assessment or has been adopted by a large number of researchers. Although results are promising and intriguing, interest in such measures appears to have diminished.

2

Theories and Models of the Disorder

2.1 Biological Models

Historically, depression has always been seen as, at least in part, somatic or biological in origin. Modern genetic studies, biochemical analyses, and scanning methods support this position. Diagnostic distinctions have been made on the basis of assumed primary biologic (endogenous) versus primarily environmentally driven (exogenous) depressions. Modern theories of the nature of the biological contribution have evolved over the last few decades as investigative research techniques have evolved.

2.1.1 Genetics

The degree to which genetics contribute to the occurrence of a disorder is studied by three primarily methodologies. Family studies start with a patient proband and identify the percentage of relatives of varying degree who also have the disorder. The studies are relatively easy to do, but do not separate the effects of genetics from the effects of shared environments. Twin studies compare the co-twins of proband twins who have the disorder. Monozygotic co-twins who share 100% of genetic material should be twice as likely to have the disorder as dizygotic co-twins who share 50% of genetic material. In these studies, environments are relatively constant, so a purer assessment of genetics is possible. In adoption studies, the children of ill parents who are adopted at a young age are compared to children who grow up with their biological parents. If they have the same elevated rates of the disorder, then genetics rather than environment is assumed to be responsible.

Genetic studies indicate that depression has a genetic component that interacts with the environment to produce the disorder

All three methodologies support the presence of a genetic component to depression. The precise estimates of the accounted-for variance vary considerably, but it is generally agreed that genetics are a significant, but not substantial, contributor that accounts for less than 50% of occurrence. Shared environment seems to play a relatively small role, whereas individual life events contribute significantly. *The genetic contribution is greater for more severe, recurrent, melancholic, or psychotic depressions.* A major role of genetics appears to be to increase the impact of negative life events in precipitating episodes of depression. Genetics provide the biological diathesis or vulnerability that interacts with environmental stress.

Studies comparing the heritability of bipolar versus unipolar depression find that *the genetic component of bipolar is greater than that for unipolar disorder.* In the families of bipolar probands, both bipolar and unipolar relatives are common. In contrast, primarily unipolar relatives are found in the families of unipolar probands. It is generally agreed that both disorders involve multiple genes, i.e., neither is due to a single dominant or recessive gene. The difference between bipolar and unipolar families has been taken to mean that the two disorders share some genes, but it may require a greater concentration of genes to produce bipolar disorder. Thus, in bipolar families you find more ill relatives, some with high concentrations of genes and some with low concentrations. In unipolar families where probands have lower concentrations, only unipolar relatives with low concentrations are likely.

2.1.2   Monoamine Hypotheses

Early biological models of depression assumed that the deficiencies in the neurotransmitters affected by antidepressant medications were the cause of depression

The idea that mental illness is the result of chemical imbalances in the brain arose from studies of the effects and mechanisms of action for medications on specific disorders. Deficiencies in neurotransmitters were hypothesized to be the basis of disorders when medications were found to increase the neurotransmitter levels. The monoamines are a group of neurotransmitters that contain a single amino group connected to a two-carbon chain. Monoamines are derived from amino acids interacting with thyroid hormones. In the 1950s and 1960s, researchers associated the neurotransmitters norepinephrine and serotonin with depression, and dopamine with schizophrenia. The idea that monoamine neurotransmitters were implicated in depression was referred to as the *monoamine hypothesis*. The earliest antidepressants were the tricyclics (Table 7), so named because their molecular structures contain three rings of atoms. The tricyclics, such as imipramine, amitriptyline, and clomipramine, increased the presence of norepinephrine and serotonin in the synapse by inhibiting their reuptake. Some of these tricyclics also influenced dopamine and other neurotransmitters as well.

Tricyclics were the first generation of antidepressants

SSRIs were the second generation of antidepressants and have largely replaced the tricyclics

The next generation of medications for depression was more selective in their effect and produced fewer side effects. Among these medications are the selective serotonin reuptake inhibitors (SSRIs, Table 8), and the selective serotonin and norepinephrine reuptake inhibitors (SNRIs, Table 9). An interesting variation on the neurotransmitter theory has been proposed in a book

Table 7
Tricyclic Antidepressants

Generic Name	Trade Name
amitriptyline	Elavil
clomipramine	Anafranil
desipramine	Norpramin
doxepin	Sinequan
imipramine	Tofranil
nortriptyline	Pamelor
trimipramine	Surmontil

Table 8
SSRIs

Generic Name	Trade Name
citalopram	Celexa
escitalopram	Lexapro
fluoxetine	Prozac
fluvoxamine	Luvox
paroxetine	Paxil
sertraline	Zoloft

Table 9
SNRIs

Generic Name	Trade Name
venlafaxine	Effexor
desvenlafaxine	Pristiq
sibutramine	Meridia
nefazodone	Serzone
milnacipran	Dalcipran
duloxetine	Cymbalta

by Parker and Manicavasagar (2005) of the University of New South Wales. These authors propose an alternative conceptualization of clinical depression as consisting of three levels. The mildest is nonmelancholic depression characterized primarily by depressed mood. Second is melancholic depression, which they see as having psychomotor disturbance as its central distinguishing feature and as potentially being either unipolar or bipolar. At the most severe is psychotic depression characterized by its psychotic features. The variation on the neurotransmitter approach is to identify nonmelancholic depression as due primarily to deficiencies in serotonin, whereas melancholic depression involves the additional complication of increasing norepinephrine involvement. Finally, dopamine involvement is added to the mix in psychotic depression. They recommend different treatment approaches characterized especially by different medication approaches for the three levels of disorder. Their full theory also looks at interactions with personality dimensions with psychotherapy, and it provides management suggestions for types of depression associated with different personality types.

Today, monoamine hypotheses as theories of depression are seen as somewhat simplistic. They do not do justice to the many interconnected systems affected in depression. Many additional neurotransmitters may be involved, and drugs that affect many different systems seem to influence depression. It is also not clear why, when neurotransmitter levels are elevated with medications, several weeks are required before clinical improvement is seen.

SNRIs are the third generation of antidepressants

2.1.3   Neuroendocrine Models

Another way of looking at the nervous system as it affects depression is to examine the functioning of the neuroendocrine system. People who have diseases of the endocrine glands often present with depressive symptoms. In particular, the hypothalamic–pituitary–adrenal (HPA) axis and cortisol secretion have been a focus of interest. The HPA axis involves a complex set of interconnections between brain neurotransmitters, certain hormones, and various organs. Response to stress involves the neurotransmitters (serotonin, norepinephrine, and others) and also involves the pituitary gland, which produces adrenocorticotropic hormone (ACTH), which in turn stimulates the adrenal gland to produce cortisol. Cortisol is a hormone that regulates various arousal and activation functions in the sympathetic nervous system. In the blood stream, one of its functions is to act as a homeostatic mechanism preventing excessive or prolonged arousal to stress.

The dexamethasone suppression test was at first thought to be a reliable biological marker of depression, but cortisol levels appear to be more complex

Cortisol levels are generally elevated in depressed individuals and return to normal levels following a depressive episode. Administration of a synthetic form of cortisol, dexamethasone, suppresses cortisol secretion in normals. In depressed persons, however, cortisol levels rapidly return to elevated levels. This phenomenon, referred to as *dexamethasone nonsuppression*, was initially believed to be a biological marker for a biological form of depression likely to respond best to medication. The test is associated with more severe forms of depression. However, it is not specific to depression, and its results are influenced by many other factors, such as alcohol and drug use, weight loss, and older age, making it insufficient in sensitivity or specificity to be considered a biological marker. It also does not predict medication response. Although the HPA axis is implicated in depression, the exact role is unclear.

2.1.4   Brain-Derived Neurotrophic Factor

One of the newest ways of looking at the biological basis of depression sees BDNF as regulating brain cell growth

Not too long ago, it was thought that neural networks were fixed and unchangeable, that neurons might die, but new neurons could never be generated. However, over the past two decades, that view has completely changed. The nervous system is now seen as having considerable plasticity. As we learn and experience our environments, neurons are pruned, growth occurs, synapses are reformed, and cells are replaced. Brain-Derived Neurotrophic Factor (BDNF) is a neuropeptide neurotransmitter that plays a substantial role in the regulation of these processes. BDNF has been found to be important in the formation of episodic (personal) and emotional memory, and it impacts the functioning of the hypothalamic–pituitary–adrenal (HPA) axis. The psychological effects of stress may be mediated in part by BDNF, which inhibits nerve growth. Depressed persons show decreased BDNF activity and inhibited nerve growth, particularly in the hippocampus, leading to reduced hippocampal volume. Antidepressants appear to stimulate BDNF and activity and growth of both new nerve cells and of the glial cells that support them. The study of BDNF and its functions is leading to a promising new "neurogenesis hypothesis" of depression.

2.1.5   Biological Rhythms

Another approach to understanding the biological basis of behavior is to look at biological rhythms. Circadian rhythms are normal biological and behavioral patterns that mark a 24-hour day–night cycle. Sleep patterns, body temperature, and other biological fluctuations are timed to a circadian cycle. For some depressed persons, various aspects of the cycle seem to be out of alignment. For example, early morning awakening and symptoms that are worse in the morning are common in depression. Studies of sleep structure also reveal abnormalities in some depressed persons. In addition to early, middle, and morning insomnias, decreased slow-wave sleep is detected in sleep-lab studies of depressed individuals. One of the more robust biological markers for depression is a reduced latency for the onset of rapid eye movement (REM) sleep. In normal individuals, REM sleep first occurs after a cycle of deep sleep an hour or more after falling asleep. In contrast, in many depressed persons, REM sleep occurs in well under an hour. REM latency is relatively stable and is not correlated with treatment response.

There are a number of indications that depression is related to a dysregulation of circadian rhythms

It has been hypothesized that early morning awakening, sleep-phase disturbances, and abnormal cortisol cycles all represent a "phase advance" desynchronization of the circadian cycle. This desynchronization may lead to other symptoms of depression. Circadian rhythms are also related to day–night cycles and the way these cycles change with the seasons. Normal individuals experience some variation in their sleeping, eating, and activity habits during seasonal cycles. Seasonal Affective Disorder may be an extension of these biological rhythm disturbances.

The biological rhythm explanation of depression suggests it is important to intervene in establishing regular normal daily cycles of activity. Ellen Frank (2005) published a manual for what she calls Interpersonal and Social Rhythm Therapy for the psychosocial treatment of bipolar disorder. The basic approach is regularized daily activity. Circadian rhythms are regulated in part by regular events in our daily cycles. The regular times we go to bed, get up in the morning, and eat our meals are all *zeitgebers*, or time givers, that help to set our biological clocks. Bringing them under regular schedules helps to resynchronize circadian rhythms to treat mood disorder.

2.2   Psychodynamic Models

During the first half of the twentieth century, psychodynamic theory was the predominant model and conceptions of depression developed from this perspective. The classic early paper is Freud's "Mourning and Melancholia" (1925), which describes depression as a disruption of the grieving process. Losses, whether of a loved one, of a relationship, or of an important activity in one's life (e.g., a job) all represent the loss of a significant unconscious object. Mourning involves a process of adjusting to the loss. If this process does not progress normally, and grief remains unresolved, depression may result. In that the loss is of an internalized part of oneself, anger and reproach for the loss may be self-directed. Anger turned inward is the basis for the depression. In mania,

Freud viewed depression as anger turned inward

Freud speculated that the same energy may be released outward in a burst of desperation. Another early paper by Karl Abraham (1911) expressed the view that mania represented the failure of repression to contain anger and self-hatred resulting from the need to give up a sexual aim without gratification. In other words, the self-hatred that would be expressed as depression is projected outward in mania. This emphasis on anger turned inward would later be challenged because many depressions involve feelings of anger toward others.

Arieti and Bemporad see depression as a failure to internalize evaluative standards

Several theorists in the later part of the century differentiated two types of depression. Arieti and Bemporad (1980) described dependency depression as a failure to internalize evaluative standards and rely on the evaluation of others for self-esteem. In contrast, dominant-goal depression results from the internalization of stringent and demanding standards. Dependency depression results from failure to please or to maintain an important relationship, whereas dominant-goal depression results from a failure to meet one's own unrealistically high and perfectionistic standards. Readers will recognize this approach as the basis for differential assessment of subtypes of depression vulnerability. Blatt's differentiation of dependent and anaclitic depressions and Beck's sociotropic and autonomous depression express similar ideas.

The idea of a depressive personality, defined in various ways, has a long history in psychodynamic thinking. The current *DSM* contains the latest example of a conception of Depressive Personality in its appendix of diagnostic criteria needing further research. Results of research trying to identify coherent and stable depressive personality types have been mixed, at best. Research conceptualizing personality traits, such as those above, interacting with life stresses have led to a more fruitful domain of research.

2.3   Behavioral Models

In the late 1960s and early 1970s, behavioral approaches were taking a prominent place in research and thinking about treatment of psychological disorders, and this period witnessed the development of desensitization and other exposure methods for treating anxiety disorders. These methods were based on the metaphor of anxiety as a conditioned emotional response. A process studied largely in animals was applied to a human problem. Behavioral approaches were slower in addressing depression and in developing a behavioral metaphor from the learning literature for depression.

Lewinsohn: Loss or lack of response contingent reinforcement

Peter Lewinsohn was one of the first researchers to develop a reinforcement model of depression (Lewinsohn, 1974). Lewinsohn asserted that depression resulted from a loss of lack of response contingent positive reinforcement. He viewed depression as a reduction in effective or productive behavior that resulted from an environment that did not reinforce the behavior. Implicit in this model is the idea that behaviors are chained and organized by important sources of reinforcement. For example, the loss of a job leads to no longer getting up early, not reading the business news in the paper, withdrawing from business friends, etc. The reinforcements associated with one's work permeate a person's life.

Lewinsohn cites three primary ways in which people might suffer from insufficient reinforcement to maintain their behavior. First, the environment may lack reinforcement due either to the loss of a reinforcer (e.g., loss of a loved one) or as a result of living in a generally deficient and unrewarding environment (e.g., poverty). Second, people may lack the skills (social, job, etc.) to obtain sufficient reinforcement. Third, people may suffer from anxiety (typically social anxiety) that keeps them from experiencing the reinforcement that the environment offers. Each of these ways of not being reinforced leads to a different therapy strategy. For the first, activity scheduling or behavioral activation is used to increase the person's rewarding activities. Often, when people are depressed, they do not engage in behavior that was formerly rewarding. This approach returns them to those behaviors. The second problem calls for social-skill training, and the third for desensitization of the anxiety. Lewinsohn later developed a psychoeducational therapy approach that combined these therapy modules and added additional content (Lewinsohn, Antonuccio, Steinmetz-Breckenridge, & Teri, 1984). A later integrative expansion of the model (Lewinsohn, Hoberman, Teri, & Hautzinger, 1985) describes a feedback loop with predisposing characteristics (vulnerabilities and immunities) that are associated with all of the factors in the following sequence: (1) antecedents (depression-evoking events); (2) disruption of "scripted" or automatic behavior patterns; (3) reduced rate of positive reinforcement and/or increased rate of aversive experience; (4) increased self-awareness (focus on oneself, self-criticism, and negative expectancies); (5) increased dysphoria; and (6) consequences (behavioral, cognitive, emotional, somatic, and interpersonal).

2.4   Interpersonal and Social Skill Models

A number of writers have characterized depression as representing a form of deficiency in social skill. Joseph Wolpe, one of the founders of the behavior therapy movement, believed that depression was due to a lack of assertiveness in obtaining deserved rewards and pleasures. He prescribed assertiveness training for depression. Assertiveness training has been assessed in several clinical trials.

Wolpe: lack of assertiveness

Interpersonal-skill deficits in depressed persons have been studied in detail by a number of researchers. Findings include such things as the tendency of depressed individuals to turn the subject of conversation to themselves, seeking negative feedback from others, and excessive self-revelation. On the assumption that these behaviors represent the interpersonal nature of depression, Pettit and Joiner (2005) developed a treatment manual focusing on changing these depressive interpersonal behaviors. It is empirically derived from the observational literature and somewhat eclectic in its approach to changing a systematic series of problematic behaviors.

Pettit and Joiner: depressive interpersonal behavior

A related approach to depression applies this model in the interpersonal context of marriage. Research on marriages with one depressed spouse tends to show that a coercive relationship develops in which the depressed behavior of one spouse is positively reinforced by the nondepressed spouse who gives in to depressive complaints. In turn, this giving in is negatively reinforced by the depressed spouse who terminates complaints. Thus a depressive mutual interaction is maintained. Following from the assumption that depression co-occurring with marital distress requires attention to the marital relationship,

Table 10
Stages of Problem Solving

(1) problem orientation

(2) problem definition and formulation

(3) generation of alternatives

(4) decision making

(5) solution implementation and verification

(6) recycling if solution fails

(7) maintenance and generalization of skills

Beach, Sandeen, and O'Leary (1990) have described a model for conceptualizing and treating depression in the context of marriage.

Beach, Sandeen, & O'Leary: marital distress

Nezu, Nezu, and Perri (1989) have taken a broad interpersonal approach to depression under the framework of problem solving. They review research on depression and problem solving and note that depressed persons are unlikely to conceptualize difficulties in their lives as problems to be solved, rather they see them as unpleasant circumstances that must be endured. When they do perceive a problem, they are poor at generating possible solutions and at evaluating them. Thus, problem solving provides a framework for working on many interpersonal and decision-making situations in a depressed person's life. The authors view problem solving as occurring in seven stages (see Table 10).

Nezu: problem solving deficits

Primary Interpersonal Problems:
– Grief
– Role disputes
– Role transitions
– Interpersonal deficits

2.5   Interpersonal Psychotherapy

Klerman & Weissman: unresolved interpersonal problems

Interpersonal Psychotherapy (IPT) was developed with a similar focus on social interactions, but from a very different theoretical perspective. Its developers, Gerald Klerman and Myrna Weissman, were influenced by the interpersonal emphasis of such psychodynamic writers as Sullivan, Myers, and Bowlby. Psychiatrist Gerald Klerman was interested in treatments of depression and their maintenance. He had also done research on the social and interpersonal processes that precipitated depressive episodes. IPT (Klerman, Weissman, Rounsaville, & Chevron, 1984) was developed as a psychotherapy approach initially employed as a means of maintaining medication treatment effects. The therapy was based on the idea that social and interpersonal processes, such as exits from the social field, were associated with the onset of depression. Klerman's earlier work on life events lead him to identify four primary problem areas associated with the onset of depression: (1) grief, such as complicated bereavement following a death; (2) role disputes, such as conflicts with a significant other in renegotiation, dissolution, or impasse; (3) role transitions, such as change in life status (e.g., divorce, moving, retirement); and (4) interpersonal deficits, such as lack of social skills, boredom, loneliness, or a paucity of attachments. Therapy from this perspective involves identifying the focal interpersonal conflict that the person is facing and helping the person to resolve it.

2.6   Learned Helplessness

The learned helplessness theory of depression developed by Martin E. P. Seligman (1981) derived from a different tradition, the development of animal models of disorders. Seligman was doing research with dogs in an escape–avoidance learning paradigm. In this type of study, the animal is in a shuttle box with two sides separated by a low barrier. A light comes on on one side of the box, signaling that a shock will be presented through a grid in the floor in a few seconds. Typically the dog first learns by trial and error that the shock can be escaped by jumping to the other side of the box. Gradually the dog learns to avoid the shock by jumping to the other side when the light comes on before the shock. Seligman observed that when the animals had an earlier experience with unavoidable shock, they were poor at learning the escape and avoidance sequence. Some dogs just lay down and waited for the shock to be over. He termed this phenomenon "learned helplessness" and viewed it as an animal model for depression. When humans encounter uncontrollable aversive experiences they feel helpless and fail to make effective efforts to improve their lot. A number of parallels between learned helplessness and depression were cited. Seligman extended his research to humans and noted that, following an experience with an unsolvable puzzle, they were less able to succeed at a solvable problem. Their behavior in this regard was similar to the behavior of the helpless animals and was also similar to the behavior of depressed individuals.

This theory evolved into a more cognitive form (Abramson, Seligman, & Teasdale, 1978) built around the idea that humans are vulnerable to becoming helpless, and thus developing depression, if they have a depressive attributional style. A depressive attributional style involves making helpless attributions that are internal, stable, and global for negative events and external, unstable, and specific for positive events. That is, people who become depressed are prone to blame themselves for negative events and assume that the internal cause is a continuing and general tendency of theirs, and at the same time they are prone not to take credit for positive events which are likely to be seen as transient and specific chance occurrences with no implications for the future or other circumstances. A further elaboration of the attributional approach was described by Abramson, Metalsky, and Alloy (1989). They added another step to the model, hopelessness, after a helpless attribution is made for a negative life event. In some instances this sequence leads to a specific form of "hopelessness depression" in which the person generalizes their helplessness to all future events.

Seligman proposed that the learned helplessness model of depression led to four possible treatment strategies. He termed these strategies: (1) Environmental Enrichment, a condition in which therapy would make the person's environment more controllable; (2) Personal Control Training, in which therapy would teach social skills to make the person more effective and less helpless; (3) Resignation Training, in which therapy would be aimed at helping the person to give up an unrealistic goal that the person is helpless to achieve; and (4) Attributional Retraining, a condition in which therapy is aimed at modifying depressive biases in making attributions about negative and positive events. Interventions did not immediately arise from Seligman's

Seligman: learned helplessness

Abramson, Metalsky, & Alloy: Hopelessness

Treatment Strategies:
– **Environmental enrichment**
– **Personal control training**
– **Resignation training**
– **Attributional retraining**

approach, but the last strategy has been used in depression prevention interventions (Seligman, Schulman, DeRubeis, & Hollon, 1999).

2.7   The Cognitive Therapy Model

Beck: cognitive distortions Psychiatrist Aaron T. Beck was trained in the psychodynamic psychiatric tradition, but became dissatisfied with psychodynamic conceptions of depression when they failed to hold up under research scrutiny. Looking for other approaches and influenced by reading the cognitive "personal construct" ideas of George Kelly, Beck (1963) adapted the central idea that experience is filtered through our cognitive interpretations of events to produce emotional reactions. Disordered emotional conditions result from distorted interpretations of life situations. Beck viewed depression as a negative view of self, the world, and the future, which he referred to as the *negative cognitive triad*. The depressed person interprets events in terms of catastrophic loss or potential loss. Negative interpretations that a person makes of specific situations are termed "automatic thoughts" in that they are so well rehearsed that the person is scarcely aware of having them. For example, consider a situation where a person passes a colleague in the hall who is looking down and does not say anything. The depressed person's automatic thought might me "He is mad at me." This interpretation then leads to sad feelings and a sequence of depressive rumination: "What did I do wrong to make him so angry?" The depressed person does not consider more rational alternatives, such as "Something bad must have happened in his meeting with the boss this morning."

Beck identified several forms of cognitive distortions that are typical of depressed persons (Table 11). For example, *arbitrary inference* is the illogical assumption that some event is caused by oneself, as in the example above. *Maximization* and *minimization* involve exaggerating the importance of negative events and brushing off positive events. *Inexact labeling* occurs when a person gives a negative label to an event and then reacts to the label. *Emotional reasoning* involves reasoning from one's emotional state, for example, "I feel bad, therefore I must have said something stupid."

Table 11
Types of Distorted Thinking

Arbitrary Inference

Dichotomous Thinking

Emotional Reasoning

Inexact Labeling

Overgeneralization

Magnification

Minimization

Selective Abstraction

Beck's Cognitive Therapy (CT) (1963; Beck, Rush, Shaw, & Emery, 1979) involves identifying negative automatic thoughts, and collaboratively developing more rational alternatives, sometimes through experiments (e.g., "Note each interaction with your boss and see if, indeed, he is *always* critical of you"). As more automatic thoughts are identified, patterns become apparent that reveal underlying assumptions and core beliefs, such as "I never succeed in making friendships" and "I am basically an unlovable and unlikeable person." CT sessions follow a structured format that includes agenda setting, reviewing homework, seeking feedback, summarizing discussions, and assigning homework. CT is today the most studied form of psychotherapy for depression.

2.8   Self-Management

Lynn P. Rehm attempted to develop an integrative theory of depression incorporating elements from Lewinsohn, Beck, and Seligman using a self-control model as an organizing framework (Rehm, 1977). The model was adapted from Kanfer's (1970) model of self-control, which was an attempt to account for the processes that people engage in when they accomplish tasks that we attribute to self-control. Examples of self-control would include persisting in difficult behavior change, such as starting an exercise program, or resisting temptation, as in quitting smoking. Adapting to change also involves self-control processes. As described by Kanfer, people engage in behaviors that can be thought of as a three-phase feedback loop consisting of self-monitoring, self-evaluation, and self-reinforcement. Self-monitoring involves becoming more conscious of the behavior and observing it over time. This observation may be unsystematic, "I smoked a lot of cigarettes today" or very systematic, involving a record of the time and place of each cigarette smoked. Self-monitoring leads into self-evaluation. The result of the self-monitored observation is compared to a formal or informal standard, "I will stay under a pack a day this week," and results in an evaluation, "I did well and feel good about it," or "I did poorly and feel bad." The final phase of the feedback loop is self-reinforcement. Kanfer argued that people influence their own behavior just as they might influence the behavior of another person, through self-administered rewards and punishments. Again these may be informal or formal. An informal reward might be just feeling good about an accomplishment, or "patting one-self on the back." A formal contingent reward might be, "I met my smoking goals this week, so I will go to a movie on Saturday." Failure to meet a goal might lead to self-punishment, mentally "kicking oneself" or contingently staying home and cleaning out the closet. The idea is to make it more likely for the patient to succeed and/or less likely to fail in the next effort.

Self-control is a learned skill and some people are better at it, and more successful in changing habits, than others. Perceived losses that lead to depression require efforts to reestablish rewarding relationships with the environment, a self-control task. Rehm (1977) postulated that depression or depression proneness as conceptualized in part by other theorists could be seen as a series of deficits in self-control skills. Six self-control deficits were proposed (Table 12). In their self-monitoring, depressed or depression-prone persons (1) attend to

Rehm: deficits in self-control behavior

Table 12
Self-Management Deficits

Monitoring negative events to the exclusion of positive events

Monitoring immediate versus future consequences

Stringent self-evaluation standards (perfectionism)

Depressive attributions of responsibility

Insufficient contingent positive self-reinforcement

Excessive self-punishment

negative events to the relative exclusion of positive events (as in Beck's selective attention or Ferster's vigilance for negative events), and (2) attend to the immediate as opposed to the delayed consequences of events (focus on current versus long-term needs). In their self-evaluation, depressed or depression-prone people (3) set stringent self-evaluative standards (perfectionism and minimizing one's own performance), and (4) make negative attributions (as described by Seligman). In self-reinforcement, these individuals (5) lack self-reward or response-contingent positive reinforcement, which supplements external-contingent positive reinforcement, and (6) excessively self-punish, which works against self-motivation toward long-term goals. The result is difficulty in working toward long-term goals in a systematic way. Self-reinforcement supplements external reinforcement (the focus of Lewinsohn's model) in controlling behavior. As a consequence of poor or disrupted self-control behavior, depressed persons lack the long-term goals most people use to organize and direct their behavior. This may be expressed as helplessness and hopelessness about the future.

The therapy that was developed using this formulation of depression is Self-Control or Self-Management Therapy. It has been evaluated in a group psycho-educational format in which the deficits are addressed in sequence. Sessions involve homework check-in, didactic presentations by the therapist, in-session paper-and-pencil exercises to get experience with the ideas presented, and homework assignments to implement the ideas. The program has been validated by Rehm and his colleagues and in other labs and clinics (Rehm & Adams, 2009).

2.9   Concluding Comments

The various models have been translated into therapy procedures that are standardized in manuals

The theoretical models are, for the most part, the basis for differing forms of psychotherapy for depression. These models have been translated into manuals that specify the rationale, procedures, and sequences of the therapies. In some instances, manuals have been updated and additional manuals have been developed for adaptations to particular populations, e.g., adolescents or the elderly. A list of these manuals appears in the Further Reading (section 5, p. 73). Most of the therapies as described in the manuals are complex approaches that include multiple interventions in a sequence. Many component interventions are similar across manuals. Behavioral activation, for example, is a component of several forms of treatment and is a treatment in and of itself.

3

Diagnosis and Treatment Indications

3.1 Dimensions and Subtypes of Depression

Mild, subclinical forms of depression are sometime treated as a prevention strategy to avoid more debilitating levels of depression. School interventions take a psychoeducational format for teaching skills for coping with stress and avoiding depression (for an example, see Stark, 1990). Interventions have also be attempted in primary care settings by offering brief forms of treatment to patients screened for mild depression on the assumption that catching the depression early might prevent more serious depression later. Mild depression may also respond to interventions less intense and time consuming than psychotherapy. Bibliotherapy may be useful for some people. A number of manualized therapies include patient manuals, and a number of books have been written directly for public consumption. David Burns (1999) book *Feeling Good: The New Mood Therapy* is a popular example. There is an accumulating research literature validating the effectiveness of bibliotherapy for depression.

For mild depressions, educational formats including bibliotherapy may be appropriate

The *DSM* does not consider bereavement following the loss of a loved one to be depression. Rather it is to be considered a normal period of sadness inherent in the human condition. However, if the bereavement persists for more than 2 months or if it involves marked functional impairment or depressive symptoms such as morbid preoccupation with worthlessness, suicidal ideation, psychotic symptoms, or psychomotor retardation, it is considered a MDE. Unresolved grief is a common psychodynamic formulation of depression and short-term psychodynamic approaches sometimes focus on grief work. IPT focuses on grief as one of the four primary forms of interpersonal processes that trigger depression.

Bereavement is often a focus of treatment, although it is not a DSM diagnosis

Severity factors into almost all decisions about the treatment of depression. It has often been asserted that psychotherapy or medication may be equally effective for mild to moderate depression, but that for severe depression medication is the treatment of choice. However, an analysis of four studies that compared medication and CT for severely depressed individuals actually found a small, but not statistically significant advantage for CT (DeRubeis, Gelfand, Tang, & Simons, 1999). Similarly, what little evidence there is suggests that psychotherapy and medications are equally effective for melancholic depressions. However, these findings are limited. The studies reviewed were all of patients who were screened and randomized in studies of outpatients. Having worked in an inpatient setting for several years, I have seen patients who were so depressed as to be essentially unresponsive to their environment. People with catatonic depressions are not good candidates for psychotherapy. Although CT has had some success with schizophrenic

For ambulatory patients psychotherapy and medications are equally effective, even for severe depression

patients, I am not aware of any studies of psychotherapy with psychotic depression.

Severe depression, as indicated by a variety of onset and course factors, tends to be more difficult to treat. In general, poorer outcomes for both psychotherapies and pharmacotherapy have been found with earlier onset, more gradual onset, more episodes, greater chronicity, double depression, incomplete remission between episodes, greater functional impairment, and more endogenous/melancholic symptoms. Reactive onset tends to predict better response to treatment, as does good social support.

Chronic depression has been successfully treated by a specific form of cognitive behavior therapy

There has been relatively little research on psychotherapy for chronic depression and Dysthymia, the chronic mild form of depression. A large study (Keller et al., 2000) compared a new form of psychotherapy, termed the Cognitive Behavior Analysis System of Psychotherapy (McCullough, 2000), to medication in the treatment of chronic depression, primarily chronic MDD alone, with Dysthymia, or with incomplete remissions. The study demonstrated separate effects for the psychotherapy and the medication, whether provided separately or in combination. Medication had a greater effect in the first 4 weeks of treatment, whereas psychotherapy had a greater effect in the latter 8 weeks of therapy.

Light therapy is often effective in treating seasonal pattern mood disorders

Seasonal Pattern mood disorders respond to light therapy. Bright, full-spectrum light from specially designed light boxes was first used for treating circadian rhythm disorders such as delayed sleep phase syndrome, shift work sleep disorder, and jet lag. This approach to treatment aims to reset biological clocks using artificial light to adjust for changes in daily sunlight patterns. Exposure to light affects melatonin production, known to regulate sleep cycles, and also may have an effect on serotonin production. Seasonal Pattern mood disorders are similarly seen as biological rhythm disorders affected by annual changes in light cycles. Bright light, up to 10,000 lux, without harmful ultraviolet radiation is assigned for specified periods of time, typically each morning. Side effects can include nausea and headaches. In efforts to avoid side effects, even brighter light sources have been used for shorter periods of time. Exposure has shown dose effects, and brighter light or light for longer periods of time produces stronger effects. Light therapy also seems to improve response to medications for nonseasonal depression.

3.2   Personality Factors as Treatment Indicators

Personality Dimensions:
– Blatt: Perfectionism and Need for Approval
– Blatt: Introjective and Anaclitic Personalities
– Beck: Autonomous and Sociotropic Personalities

Predicting whether a particular patient will respond well to a particular treatment modality has been tried in a number of ways. Some personality factors may be useful for prognosis, i.e., they may predict whether a patient is generally a good candidate for treatment. Good social support, for example, is associated with better outcome in most forms of treatment. Other factors may be useful in matching clients to particular forms of therapy. Matches may be made on the basis of remediation, i.e., if the person has a particular pronounced deficit, then they would be matched to the treatment that remediated that deficit. For example, the sociotropic person who was particularly vulnerable to interpersonal difficulties might best be matched to an interpersonal therapy, whereas an autonomous person might be matched to a skill-building therapy. This type of match is referred to as *compensation*, where deficits are strengthened. Although seldom done, a person could also be matched to a therapy based on a particular strength. This type of match is referred to as *capitalization*. A person with good social skills to begin with might be most successful in dealing with their depression by means of a treatment program utilizing social skills.

Personality factors may be compensated for or capitalized upon

Blatt and his colleagues (Blatt, Quinlan, Pilkonis, & Shea, 1995) used data from the National Collaborative Study to examine the role of perfectionism and need for approval in the prediction of treatment outcome. These authors derived measures from subscales of the Dysfunction Attitudes Scale. They viewed perfectionism as a correlate of Blatt's concept of introjective personality or Beck's concept of autonomous personality, and need for approval as a correlate of Blatt's anaclitic personality or Beck's sociotropic personality. They found that perfectionism, rather than being a specific predictor of better response to CT, turned out to be a prognostic indicator of poor response to all forms of treatment, including imipramine. Need for approval was marginally, but nonsignificantly, related to positive outcome on some measures, but not differentially for IPT as had been predicted.

Perfectionism was found to be a general negative prognostic factor

A study by Barber and Muenz (1996) compared CT and IPT for individuals assessed on the personality dimensions of avoidance and obsessiveness. They hypothesized that clients high on avoidance would do better in CT, and those high on obsessiveness would do better in IPT. As predicted, CT was more helpful for those with high avoidance and low obsessiveness, whereas IPT was more helpful for those low in avoidance and high in obsessiveness. These researchers also found that married clients did better in CT and unmarried did better in IPT. Zettle, Haflich, and Reynolds (2006) found that sociotropic individuals did better in a group-format CT, capitalizing on their interpersonal orientation, and autonomous individuals did better in an individual format.

Avoidance versus obsessiveness, and sociotropy versus autonomy differentially predict formats outcome in different therapy

Rude and Rehm (1991) reviewed all studies that had compared cognitively oriented with behaviorally oriented treatments for depression and had assessed cognitive and behavioral deficits. These studies had virtually all predicted remediation effects, i.e., the people with more severe cognitive deficits would do better in the cognitive therapies and those with behavioral deficits would do better in the behavioral programs. However, we failed to find any evidence for remediation. What evidence was found suggested capitalization effects. One exception was that the Learned Resourcefulness Scale was a general positive prognostic indicator, although it had been predicted to be a differential predictor for CT. Therapies may be indeed capitalizing on strengths, or it might be that the short-term treatments typically offered in research trials are insufficient to treat severe deficits but may do very well when dealing with persons with only minor deficits. All depressed subjects may have some degree of deficit in both cognitive and behavioral arenas.

Cognitive versus behavioral deficits do not predict differential response to cognitive and behavioral therapies

Beutler and his colleagues (Beutler, Castonguay, & Follette, 2006; Beutler, Clarkin, & Bongar, 2000; Castonguay & Beutler, 2006), taking a much broader perspective, directed a process whereby an interassociation task force abstracted core principles associated with successful outcomes in psychotherapy research across theoretical orientations. They derived common principles applicable to psychotherapy generally and specific principles associated with clusters of disorders in the following domains: relationship, treatment, client,

Matching can be accomplished on the basis of relationship, treatment, client, and therapist factors

and therapist factors. For example, 3 of 11 client factors specific to treating depression and dysphoria follow: The therapist's use of directive therapeutic interventions should be planned to inversely correspond with the patient's manifest level of resistant traits and states; patients whose personalities are characterized by impulsivity, social gregariousness, and external blame for problems benefit more from direct behavioral change and symptom reduction efforts, including building new skills and managing impulses, than they do from procedures that are designed to facilitate insight and self-awareness; and patients whose personalities are characterized by low levels of impulsivity, indecisiveness, self-inspection, and over control tend to benefit more from procedures that foster self-understanding, insight, interpersonal attachments, and self-esteem than they do from procedures that aim at directly altering symptoms and building new social skills (Beutler, Castonguay, & Follette, 2006).

Parker and Manicavasagar (2005) drew on work they had done in temperament and personality that differentiated eight personality traits or coping styles. The eight traits are viewed as further differentiations within the five-factor model of personality. They are recognized as traits such that any individual could be describe by a profile of each of the traits, but they are also viewed as coping styles such that many individuals could be distinguished as having one of these traits as a primary coping style. These researchers take this model one step further by suggesting that when individuals develop nonmelancholic depression, their primary coping style defines a subtype of depression. The eight subtypes based on the personality traits are:

Primary coping styles may require different therapy strategies

(1) Perfectionistic;
(2) Irritable;
(3) Anxious Worrying;
(4) Social Avoidant;
(5) Personal Reserve;
(6) Rejection Sensitive;
(7) Self-Focused; and
(8) Self-Critical.

They add to this list three forms of depression based on response to stress. These are:

(9) Acute Stress Related;
(10) Acute Stress Related: Lock and Key; and
(11) Chronic Stress Related.

The idea of a "Lock and Key" response to stress is that some individuals who are repeatedly exposed to a form of stress, for example, harsh criticism from a parent, become vulnerable later on in life to similar stresses. Harsh criticism from a supervisor leads to extreme distress and depression. The key again opens the lock response.

Parker and Manicavasagar go on to make suggestions for how therapy should be adapted to each of these personality types. For the Perfectionistic subtype of depression, they suggest focusing on specific tasks and clear outcomes, problem solving and goal setting for short-term goals, and a working on long-term goals of reducing self-criticism, intolerance, and procrastination. Medication is not recommended.

For the Anxious Worrying subtype, Parker and Manicavasagar recommend a highly structured individual or group therapy focusing on reducing autonomic arousal and addressing dysfunctional thinking, with booster sessions to consolidate gains. Medication with an SSRI is indicated for these patients. Parker and Manicavasagar believe that the Rejection Sensitive individual would benefit from medium- to long-term therapy focusing on interpersonal issues, with clear goals and a termination date set at the outset. For these individuals, consideration should be given to including significant others in therapy, and possible medication with an SSRI or MAOI for atypical depression. They suggest that therapy for the Self-Focused individual should be structured and short-term. The focus should be on specific behavior-change strategies, breaking the spiral of self-destructive behavior, conflict resolution, and anger management. The individual should be helped to learn respect for the rights and property of others, and to reflect on long-term consequences of his or her behavior.

For Acute Stress-Related depression, brief, time-limited therapy is recommended with clearly stated realistic goals and a strong focus on problem-solving strategies. An SSRI could be considered. If the stress is of the "Lock and Key" type, therapy may be of medium length and the focus should be on the previous situation that evoked the same cognitions and emotions, and on insight into its origins and significance. Alternative ways of coping should be explored. An SSRI might be considered and anxiolitics should be avoided. For Chronic Stress related depression, medium- to long-term therapy is suggested with a focus on reducing exposure to stressors, support and problem solving, and challenging negative self-perceptions. Direct advice and instruction is likely to be useful, and suicide prevention may be necessary. Again, an SSRI might be considered. Although not a therapy manual, the Parker and Manicavasagar book has many useful therapy suggestions and offers an alternative and complementary way of looking at depression.

3.3   Life Events and Stress

Life events and stress influence the onset and course of depression, and this is relevant to therapy. Life-event research tends to focus on three areas: disasters, major life events, and minor life events. Disasters are catastrophic events, including natural events such as earthquakes, tornados, and hurricanes, and more personal life-threatening events, such as combat experiences, rape, and serious automobile accidents. This literature characterizes the types of immediate, medium-range, and long-term responses people have to disasters. The long-term responses include psychiatric conditions such as Post Traumatic Stress Disorder and depression. Beck defines depression as a response to loss or perception of loss. People who experience disaster may respond with grief, but they also begin to perceive the world as unsafe. People who have experienced an earthquake often speak of losing their sense that the world is a safe place. Helplessness is often induced by unpredictable catastrophic events.

Major life events are normal events that are accompanied by high stress, such as divorce, death of a loved one, losing a job, foreclosure on a mortgage, or going to jail. Major life events include positive events that are nonetheless stressful, such as birth of a child, moving into a new house, starting a new job,

Stressful life events increase risk for depression and may precipitate episodes

or taking a vacation. Major live events vary in their level of impact, and their stressful effects are cumulative.

Single events may trigger episodes of depression. Checklists of life events have been developed that yield stress indices. The best known of these is the Holmes and Rahe Stress Scale (Holmes & Rahe, 1967); this scale weights different life events experienced in the last 6 months and yields a summed risk-factor score. Accumulated stress and chronic stress are psychological- and health-risk factors for the onset of many conditions, including depression. Brown and Harris (1984) reported that the higher the number of chronic risk factors a woman had in her life, the higher her likelihood of developing depression in the face of an acute stress. Dealing with stressful major life events is often the focus of therapy for depression.

Minor life events influence daily mood

Minor life events are the daily small stressors or hassles that we all deal with, such as getting a flat tire, having an important event rained out, or bad news on television. Unpleasant events influence a person's mood in a negative direction, and pleasant events influence a person's mood in a positive direction. Scales for tracking negative and positive events have been developed and have been shown to correlate positively and negatively, respectively, with depressed mood. Each type of event contributes independently to mood and the combination correlates more highly with mood than either does alone. This well-established finding is used in various therapy programs for depression that employ behavioral activation, most notably Peter Lewinsohn's behavior therapy (P. M. Lewinsohn, Antonuccio, Steinmetz-Breckenridge, & Teri, 1984).

Childhood trauma predicted better response to psychotherapy than to medication

A unique finding regarding the effects of childhood trauma was reported by Nemeroff et al. (2003). The finding came from the large outcome study by Keller et al. (2000) that compared the antidepressant nefazodone with a the Cognitive Behavioral Analysis System of Psychotherapy (CBASP), and their combination, in the treatment of chronic depression. This paper examined the outcome of treatment for a subset of patients who had a history of childhood trauma (loss of parents at an early age, physical or sexual abuse, or neglect). Whereas, in the overall study, the medication and psychotherapy were equally effective and the combination was superior to either alone, for this subset of patients psychotherapy was superior to medication and the combination was only marginally superior to psychotherapy alone. The authors suggest that, for depressed individuals with childhood trauma, psychotherapy may be an essential element of treatment.

4

Treatment

4.1   Methods of Treatment

4.1.1   Therapy Packages

One of the major developments in the treatment of depression over the last several decades has been the codifying of treatment procedures into therapy manuals. As new theories of depression have been developed, therapy procedures that follow from the theory have been worked out and examined in research trials. It has become a standard part of this process to write a manual in sufficient detail that others can replicate the therapy with a minimum amount of training.

Virtually all of these therapies are package programs. They are made up of therapy components that are presented in sequence in the manuals. I have tried to give a sense of these components in my earlier discussion of theories of therapy. Many components of therapy may be developed from a particular theory. In addition, manuals often contain elements that are not necessarily associated with a particular theory, but are helpful topics to be covered in dealing with depression, such as reviewing the symptoms of depression in an early session. Manuals also contain procedures that have more to do with the structure of therapy sessions than with the content of the theory from which the therapy is derived. For example, manuals may include recommendations for review of homework, agenda setting, or reviewing topics covered in therapy. Nearly all of these therapies are psychoeducational or partly psychoeducational in nature. They teach the patient about the nature of depression as viewed by the particular theory and may introduce a set of constructs and a vocabulary to explicate the therapy.

> **Manualized therapies are complex treatment packages**

Therapy manuals share many similar elements with different rationales and theoretical origins. Also, some elements are recommended in one manual and discouraged in another. In one manual the therapist is encouraged to grant the patient the sick role, whereas in another the sick role is discouraged. In one manual childhood history of the client is explored extensively, whereas in others the therapist is advised to avoid the topic. One manual has the patient self-monitor situations in which they feel particularly bad, and another has them monitor positive events. Therapists of any orientation who read widely and who may want to draw from a variety of manuals understandably find this confusing and discouraging.

> **Manuals share similar elements**

Manuals also tend, in part, to be "one size fits all" programs. Although components may be adapted to the individual, the same components are applied to everyone. In a social-skills component, the individual's interpersonal problems may be identified and form the basis of role-play exercises, and in a goal-setting component, individuals select the goals they want to work on in their lives. Nevertheless, all are receiving social-skill training and goal setting.

Although the empirical literature on matching does not yield evidence of matching effects, in the sense of matching behavior-therapy elements to individuals with behavioral deficits and cognitive-therapy element to those with cognitive deficits, it makes sense to use the program components that fit the client's problems. Depression clients vary immensely in symptom patterns, in the life events and daily hassles they are facing, in the interpersonal environments and problems they face, and in their personal skills and coping styles.

Therapy components   In this chapter, rather than review the brand-name therapies as packages, I am going to attempt to review components of therapy and discuss what one can learn from the ways in which the components are handled by different therapies. I will give examples of the types of presenting problems to which these components are likely to best apply. To some extent I will also discuss the logic of sequencing components and elements of therapy for depression. My intent is not to present a new therapy package program drawn from other programs, but simply to identify basic therapy components that can be abstracted from different therapies. *Any therapist who is competent in these components could treat most depressions competently.* Most of these components are also applicable in doing therapy for other problems, but they have a particular place in the array of techniques that are applicable to depression.

Relationship factors are important in all forms of psychotherapy. Building rapport, establishing trust, and establishing a working alliance with the person that includes agreement on a clear set of goals, are all important as a basis for therapy. These factors are generic to all forms of therapy. My goal here is to describe and discuss therapy components that are most relevant to depression, even though they, too, may have wider applicability.

4.1.2   Education About Depression

Education about depression is a common first step in therapy   A number of therapy manuals include in a first session a discussion of the symptoms of depression. This seems like a natural place to start therapy, and it may have therapeutic value in a number of ways. Research suggests that if you ask someone to identify the symptoms of depression, they can do a fairly good job, but when you ask them to judge whether they themselves or someone they know well is depressed, they have a much harder time putting the pieces together. So the first effect of such an educational exercise may be to help people see that the parts of what they are experiencing are connected under the broad umbrella of depression. In our self-management therapy groups I have often heard clients say, "I haven't wanted to call up my friends lately, but I did not realize that it was part of my depression," or "I have had that tired feeling, too, but it did not occur to me that it was part of depression."

Clients also learn that they are not alone, and that depression is a syndrome shared by many people. Clients often feel that they are the only ones to experience what they are going through, and believe no one else could understand what it is like to be them. Education helps patients understand that many people have these experiences, and that others can understand them.

Education also includes a discussion of the causes of depression. Many individuals come to therapy with misconceptions about the causes of depression. It is not unusual for clients to have read or seen media accounts that say depression is a "biological imbalance" or a "brain disease." Other common conceptions are that depression is a response to stress, or it is solely the product of maladaptive thinking. Some people come in with psychodynamic ideas about childhood problems in their upbringing or religious ideas about punishment for their sins. It is a good idea to review a biopsychosocial model to give patients a more realistic view and help them understand that depression has multiple causes.

Biology represents only one set of causes. Genetics does make some individuals more prone to depression, and changes in brain chemistry and physiology occur in depression, although it is not clear whether they are cause or effect. Psychology represents a second set of causes. A pessimistic outlook, low self-esteem, and a sense of powerlessness are some of the tendencies that may contribute to depression. Many of these tendencies may be acquired though experiences early in life. The environment, especially the social environment, represents another set of causal factors in depression. Negative life events, losses, or prolonged stresses can precipitate depression. Some forms of depression may be more biological, some more psychological, and some more environmental, but most depressions are caused by some combination of the above factors.

At another level, people can be educated about normal mood and what influences it on a day-to-day basis. Again, biology is only one factor. Feeling tired or distressed can lead to a down mood. The environment is a contributor, but environment affects our mood by the way we behave in response to an event or how we perceive and think about the event. Thus, biology, behavior, and thinking influence mood directly. The idea of therapy can be introduced from this perspective. Mood can be improved though changes in biology, as with rest or medication. Mood can also be influenced by changes in behavior and changes in thinking. Psychotherapy uses the latter two routes to change mood and thus treat depression.

Introducing a biopsychosocial model is important

Mood is influenced by behavior, thinking, and biology

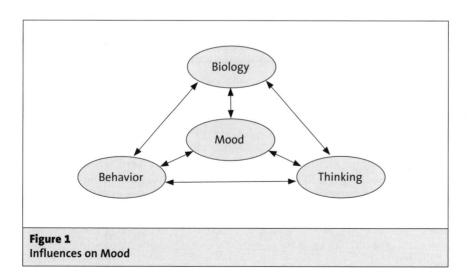

Figure 1
Influences on Mood

Figure 1 illustrates this idea. Mood, biology, behavior, and thinking all influence one another, but we cannot intervene on mood directly. We can only influence mood through changes in biology, behavior, or thinking.

An educational introduction can go a long way toward relieving what is sometimes referred to as "depression about depression," i.e., being depressed about not being able to do anything about one's depression. Many people feel that they should be able to overcome their depression by willpower alone, and people are often told by others that they should just "shake it off." Being depressed to many people means that they are bad, crazy, damaged, inadequate, punished, worthless, or unlovable. Teaching clients that depression is a common experience, with known symptoms and causes, can alleviate these feelings and instill optimism for change.

4.1.3   Behavioral Activation

Behavioral activation is often a top priority in treatment planning

Behavioral activation is the therapy strategy of assigning the depressed client specific activities to increase his or her engagement in pleasurable and rewarding experiences. It is a strategy employed in a number of forms of therapy. Behavioral activation is central to Lewinsohn's behavior therapy for depression (Lewinsohn, Antonuccio, Steinmetz-Breckenridge, & Teri, 1984). Other examples of its incorporation into therapy approaches include Beck's recommendation that it should be a starting point in therapy, if necessary (Beck, Rush, Shaw, & Emery, 1979), and my use of it as an initial phase of Self-Management Therapy (Rehm & Adams, 2009). Behavioral activation has also come to be used as a therapy for depression in and of itself (Martell, Addis, & Jacobson, 2002).

The rationale for behavioral activation can be derived from Lewinsohn's model of depression as "a loss of lack of response contingent reinforcement" (Lewinsohn, Hoberman, Teri, & Hautzinger, 1985). Behavioral activation puts depressed persons back into activities that are rewarding, and it is assumed that the rewards associated with these activities will maintain nondepressive behavior. From a cognitive point of view, putting the person into rewarding situations may also improve mood, which in turn may reduce negative thinking.

Lewinsohn devised the Pleasant Events Schedule (PES) to help depressed persons identify activities that they used to find pleasurable, but which they were no longer doing on a regular basis. In my Self-Management Therapy program, participants monitor positive activities daily and note which activities are associated with elevated mood on a given day. Beck distinguishes between

Pleasurable events bring immediate reward, whereas mastery events bring delayed reward

pleasure and mastery events. Pleasure events are immediately rewarding with positive feelings (e.g., eating ice cream, or having an enjoyable conversation with someone). Mastery events accomplish something that will lead to reward later (e.g., finishing the dishes right after dinner so one has time for a relaxing evening, or sending out Christmas cards and anticipating receiving cards back from friends). The difference is essentially immediate versus delayed reward. It is usually better in behavioral activation to start with pleasure events and work up to mastery events. It is also a good idea to encourage social activities for sociotropic individuals and accomplishment activities for autonomous individuals.

When the rationale for the intervention has been presented and target activities have been identified, it is important to specify when and where the person is going to engage in the activity. Daily schedules are useful for this purpose. As your client increases his or her pleasant activities, assignments of increasing number and effort can be scheduled.

4.1.4   Scheduling as an Intervention

Behavioral activation involves scheduling rewarding activities, but scheduling has a broader use in time management. Some depressed persons are receiving inadequate reinforcement because they are too busy to do anything that is rewarding or personally satisfying. Consider the working woman who also does the cooking and cleaning and drives the children to school and to after-school and weekend activities. She may have no time to herself or to spend with friends. Busy people often feel overwhelmed, disorganized, and not in control of their lives.

Behavioral activation often requires a focus on scheduling and time management

Scheduling in such instances usually starts with making out a schedule for a typical week. Writing out a schedule may help the person to see that he or she really is overcommitted, and that it is necessary to set priorities and make choices. After a more realistic schedule has been established, it may be important to make doing something enjoyable a priority and therapists may have to help clients make choices that will support these positive activities.

Scheduling activities improves response-contingent positive reinforcement, and it also may help the person feel more in control and therefore less helpless. Other uses of scheduling will be described in the discussion of social rhythm therapy, and in self-management goal setting discussed below.

4.1.5   Continuous Assessment

Many forms of therapy, especially behavioral and cognitive therapies, stress the importance of continuous assessment. Assessment takes multiple forms and fills multiple purposes. First, symptom assessment is important. Overall progress of treatment can best be assessed by periodic reassessments with simple symptom checklists. In our Self-Management Program, for example, we give participants the Beck Depression Inventory at every other session. For the therapist, it provides a gauge of progress. It can also be a warning that things are not going well and that special attention needs to be given to the problems of a particular patient. The suicide item is especially important for the therapist to monitor. Repeating the test gives the client feedback and may highlight areas of improvement or of worsening.

Continuous assessment is valuable for evaluating effectiveness and can be an intervention in and of itself

Other forms of assessment are built into therapies. Daily mood ratings that are done along with self-monitoring exercises provide feedback to therapist and client. Participants monitor pleasant events in Lewinsohn's program and positive activities in our Self-Management Program. Monitoring mood demonstrates to participants that what they do and what they think influences their mood. They may also note trends over time in average weekly mood ratings. It is also important to note that self-monitoring is reactive. Things you want to increase tend to increase when they are monitored, and things you want to decrease actually decrease. Continuous assessment is an intervention as well as a simple feedback mechanism.

4.1.6   Skill Training

Skill training can take a number of forms

Skill training as an intervention takes a number of forms. It is included as a strategy in a number of therapy manuals with a variety of rationales. Lewinsohn viewed a lack of social skills as one way in which a person might be deficient in obtaining response-contingent positive reinforcement. His group tried various forms of group therapy with feedback from others in the group as a strategy to improve the verbal social skills of the participants.

Assertiveness involved learning to assert one's rights appropriately

Joseph Wolpe (1958) believed that lack of assertiveness was a basis for depression. He described cases he treated using **assertiveness training**. He and the client role played various problematic situations with instruction and feedback to improve the client's skills. Assertiveness training has been evaluated in randomized trials in individual (Bellack, Hersen, & Himmelhoch, 1981) and group formats (Rehm, Fuchs, Roth, Kornblith, & Romano, 1979), although in neither of these studies did the assertion program outperform contrast conditions. In either format, therapy consists of instructions, role playing, feedback, modeling, positive reinforcement, and homework assignments. Participants bring in situations that they have had difficulty with during the week and/or therapists may supply typical difficult assertion situations (e.g., returning an item to a store, complaining about poor service in a restaurant). Very specific skills and strategies are typically the focus of role plays. Establishing eye contact, body posture, gestures, facial expression, voice tone, inflection and volume, and timing are attended to, as well as specific forms of content. A content example might be that, when trying to return an item to a store, first make a clear, firm statement of the situation and what you want the person to do. If, in response, the store clerk avoids a direct response and starts citing the store's return policies, the client might be encouraged to repeat the simple request over and over (a strategy referred to as "broken record"). Assertion training typically stresses the difference between nonassertive, assertive, and aggressive responses as a matter of the appropriate moderation.

Conversation skills may give a person confidence in social situations

Simple **conversation skills**, such a making small talk at a party, can be a related focus of skill training. Depression is often accompanied by poor self-esteem, evaluation anxiety, and other symptoms of social anxiety. Depressed people often avoid social situations in which they fear they may be looked down upon, embarrassed, or otherwise make a bad impression. The same role-playing format is used with a similar focus on verbal and nonverbal behavior in problematic social situations. Content strategies include such things as having a list of potential conversation topics prepared in advance before attending a party.

4.1.7   Problem Solving

Problem solving involves a set of skills that cover a number of issues relevant to depression. Nezu, Nezu, and Perri (1989) view problem solving as an umbrella concept for many skill deficits. They review evidence that depressed people are poor at solving laboratory and real-life problems. In fact, depressed people tend not to identify problematic situations as problems, but rather see them as unpleasant situations that they have to endure. This tendency is similar in many ways to the phenomenon of learned helplessness. Problem solving, as a therapy strategy, begins with teaching depressed persons to identify and define problems in their lives. This is followed by generating multiple possible solutions to the problem without judgment. General solutions are encouraged. Next, each solution is evaluated for its potential to solve the problem. This may involve generating specific tactics that might be ways to enact the general strategy. It also involves estimating the probability that the tactic can be carried out and will work. After a best potential strategy is identified, the depressed person is encouraged to try it out, get feedback, evaluate its effectiveness, and then continue, modify, or change to a new tactic or strategy.

Problem solving skills are often deficient in depression

4.1.8   Interpersonal Psychotherapy

IPT (Klerman, Weissman, Rounceville, & Chevron, 1984), which derives from a psychodynamic perspective, also takes a skill-building approach to specific forms of interpersonal issues. The four primary issues are (1) grief, (2) role disputes, (3) role transitions, and (4) interpersonal deficits. These targets bear some similarities to the targets of other skill-oriented approaches. Role disputes and interpersonal deficits might be approached by the problem-solving and skill-training strategies described above. Grief and role transitions are similar to the targets of self-management of change and goal setting to be described below.

IPT focuses on specific interpersonal issues

In contrast to the therapies discussed so far, IPT uses therapeutic strategies drawn from the interpersonally oriented psychodynamic approach, such as encouraging expression of emotions in sessions and use of the therapeutic relationship. For cases where grief is the focus, IPT stresses relating the client's symptom onset to the death of a significant other. The relationship with the deceased is reconstructed and the sequence and consequences of events surrounding the death are explored. Finally, IPT moves the person on to considering other ways to become involved with people.

When role disputes are the focus of treatment, the therapist attempts to relate symptom onset to overt or covert disputes with a significant other. A determination is made of the stage of the dispute and whether renegotiation is possible or whether the dispute is at an impasse and dissolution of the relationship should be considered. The therapist helps the patient understand how nonreciprocal role expectations relate to the dispute and whether there are parallels in other relationships. The therapist and client also examine the ways in which disputes in the person's life have been perpetuated.

In dealing with depression stemming from role transitions, depressive symptoms are related to the transition and to the attendant difficulties in coping. Positive and negative aspects of both the old and new roles are reviewed and feelings about loss and change itself are explored. The person is encouraged to appropriately release the affect surrounding the losses involved, but to realistically evaluate what is lost and explore opportunities in the new role.

The person is encouraged to develop new sources of social support and new skills for the new role.

Dealing with interpersonal deficits involves relating depressive symptoms to problems of social isolation and lack of fulfillment. Past significant relationships are reviewed, including both negative and positive aspects. Repetitive relationship patterns are explored, and positive and negative feelings about the therapist are discussed to see if parallels exist with other relationships.

Overcoming depressive habits involves undoing behaviors that may put off others

A final skill-training approach is based on the research literature that examines the way in which depressed persons actually interact with others. Findings suggest that depressed persons engage in a number of behaviors that perpetuate their depression and distance them from others. This strategy involves **overcoming depressive habits**. Pettit and Joiner (2005) used the literature on the observed behavior of depressed people to develop a series of exercises to help people change their behavior and improve coping skills. Some of these are the same as in the other social-skill approaches, including learning better verbal and nonverbal skills and being more assertive. Others are more novel topics and include correcting depressive habits such as self-handicapping or selling oneself short to others, the habit of seeking negative feedback, dependency on others, and the impact of depressive behavior on others.

The Pettit and Joiner book is written as either a self-help book or a workbook to be used in conjunction with a therapist. It offers the rationale for examining each depressive habit, examples to understand it better, exercises to assess whether it is true of the particular person, and ways to explore alternative behaviors. Clients are given homework assignments that require them to try out the new behaviors and strategies. Homework typically consists of monitoring the behavior in question and experimenting with alternative ways of responding to situations.

4.1.9   Countering Helplessness

Helplessness may be countered by a number of skill-building strategies

Many of the skill training strategies not only increase positive reinforcement but also help the person feel more in control and overcome learned helplessness. In fact, skill training is one of the four general therapy strategies that Seligman (1981) suggests for overcoming helplessness. A second strategy is environmental control, which refers to putting the person in a more controllable environment. Scheduling and time management help achieve this goal. Seligman's third strategy is resignation training, i.e., helping the person give up an unattainable and unrealistic goal. This might occur in many forms of therapy.

The most novel of Seligman's strategies is to teach the person to make less depressive attributions for the causes of events in their lives. In the attributional formulation of helplessness, depressed people make internal, stable, and specific attributions for negative events; i.e., they attribute the cause of the negative event to themselves, to something enduring about themselves, and to a general quality that produces the same negative results in other situations. For positive events, the depressive attributions are external, unstable, and specific; i.e., they are credited to an external source that has no implication for future success and is limited to this event only. In sum, *helplessness results from blaming oneself for bad things and not taking any credit for good things.*

Attributions for Positive and Negative Events Exercise

Positive event: Completed a crossword puzzle.

Depressed cause: "It was easy."

Why is this a depressed cause? *Attributes to external, unstable, specific cause.*

Better: "I am pretty good at crossword puzzles."

Why is this better? *Takes credit but is specific to crossword puzzles.*

Even better: "I am pretty smart."

Why is this even better? *Realistic if you regularly complete the puzzles.*

Negative event: I expressed an opinion and my friend disagreed with me.

Depressed cause: "No one ever respects my opinion."

Why is this a depressed cause? *It is my fault (internal), everyone treats me this way (general), and it will always be that way (stable).*

Better: "Maybe I was wrong this time."

Why is this better? *Takes blame (internal) but assumes it is specific and unstable.*

Even better: "My opinion is okay, too."

Why is this even better? *He can have his own opinion (external), and that doesn't mean that he will be right in other situations (specific) or at other times in the future (unstable).*

Attribution retraining involves teaching depressed persons what a negative attribution is for both negative and positive events, and then teaching them to question these attributions and to consider more realistically positive attributions. They learn to take at least some credit for positive events and not to take all the blame for negative events. In my Self-Management Therapy program, we use a series of examples beginning with examples of negative attributions with varying degrees of more positive attributions. Then we have participants fill in depressed and nondepressed attributions for hypothetical events. The homework assignment that follows requires that clients identify attributions for events made during the week and think of and record more positive attributions.

Attribution retraining has been used in therapy trials

4.1.10 Cognitive Techniques

CT, originated by Aaron Beck (1972), views depression as the product of irrational beliefs that underlie interpretations of daily events. Along with the lack of reward (skill deficit) metaphor, and the helplessness metaphor, the cognitive metaphor has been one of the three ways of looking at depression that have guided most depression research for the last three decades. Beck defined depression as consisting of a cognitive triad of a negative view of the self, of the world, and of the future. Negative interpretations occur when negative schemas acquired in childhood resurface when an event evokes feelings similar to those felt in childhood. These negative schemas then color the person's interpretations of self, world, and future. *CT consists of strategies for making the person aware of the irrationality of the negative interpretations they are making.*

The cognitive view of depression is that it is based on negative distortions of events based on underlying beliefs

CT sessions have a distinct structure. Early in the session, the therapist and client set an agenda for the session. Collaboration in this process is stressed. It is the therapist's job to keep the session focused on the agenda, but also to pause along the way and make sure that the client is still in agreement about the agenda, which may be amended as needed. The therapist also offers summaries of where they are in the agenda and what has been accomplished. At each of these points the therapist seeks feedback from the client. Near the end of the session, an overall summary is given, feedback is sought, and homework for the week is collaboratively established. The therapeutic relationship is characterized as **collaborative empiricism**, i.e., the therapist acts as a collaborator with the client in testing the client's interpretations against reality through logical examination and behavioral experiments. During the session, the therapist engages in Socratic questioning to help the client examine the logic of inferences they might be making. What is the evidence for the conclusion? What alternative conclusions are possible? What is the likelihood that one of the other interpretations is more accurate? Small experiments may also be employed in homework assignments to test assumptions. What would happen if you smiled and said "good morning" to the neighbor who you think does not like you?

> **The relationship between therapist and patient is one of collaborative empiricism**

Beck describes these irrational interpretations of events as **automatic thoughts**. They are automatic because the person is typically not aware of the assumptions he or she is making. Various formats of self-monitoring can be used to bring up these thoughts during therapy. When the depressed person

---

Clinical Vignette
Structuring Sessions and Lives

I used to think of the structuring of sessions in cognitive therapy as a somewhat independent component of the overall therapy. It was good to keep sessions organized, but I believed this had little to do with the content of the cognitive distortions that were being examined. I have come to see that it is quite integral to the process. For many people, structuring provides a lesson in organizing their thinking in ways that lead to practical solutions. Previously, these depressed clients tended to view each adverse situation as an unavoidable obstacle that they had unfortunately encountered. They were willing to talk about these situations, but essentially did nothing but wait for their circumstances to change.

The idea of identifying an adverse situation as a problem to solve (see problem solving, above), agreeing to put it on the agenda for the day's session, sticking to the topic, pausing occasionally to discuss the progress being made, and hearing a summary back from the therapist about progress, can be an important lesson in metacognition, i.e., how to think about a problem and work it through. This is a new experience for many people and one of the most important lessons they take away from treatment.

A practicum client in our training clinic with a long history of prior therapy began to tell her therapist about a long-standing problem with her son. The therapist asked if she wanted to discuss this as the agenda for the day, helped her decide exactly what she was looking for in the situation, and identified her alternatives. At the end of the session, the client commented about the amount of time she had spent complaining about the past and what a waste it had been in comparison to the last hour spent identifying potential solutions to her problems with her son.

responds to a situation with negative feelings, he or she is encouraged to write down the feeling and the situation in which it occurred. Then the person is instructed to try to identify the automatic thought that connects the situation to the feeling. As the client gets better at disputing automatic thoughts, she may also be asked to write down alternate, and more rational, thoughts on the monitoring form. Monitoring forms may be quite complex, with ratings of the degree of the negative mood, how strongly the person believes the automatic thought, and how these change when alternatives are considered.

A client of mine recorded a situation in which she was having a conversation at lunch with a colleague about a play they had both seen. The client had given her opinion of the play and the colleague had offered a very different opinion. After lunch the client felt despondent and depressed. She identified the automatic thought as "She does not respect me, because she did not agree with my opinion." Further exploration led to identifying a key underlying assumption, "I must be correct in everything I say or do or people will not respect me." Putting this together with other assumptions ultimately led to the core belief that "If I don't keep up a perfect façade, people will see that I am really worthless." This process of looking for the assumption underlying the assumption is part of the process of CT. Core beliefs may be woven into a more complex set of schemas about oneself; these schemas are often derived from early experiences.

Therapy progresses from identifying distorted automatic thoughts to finding the assumptions that underlie them and the core beliefs that hold them together

4.1.11 Mindfulness

Mindfulness is a relatively new concept in the field of psychotherapy. It is drawn in part from Eastern philosophy and is often seen as an extension or maintenance phase that is added to CT to prevent relapse. Mindfulness involves a concentrated focus on the present and a nonjudgmental acceptance of thoughts and feelings. Ordinary mental life shifts focus from present to future and past. These shifts are believed to engender negative thinking for the depressed person. Mindfulness prevents the reoccurrence of negative thinking by countering rumination about past or future. Mindfulness is used as a tool to help clients step away from their ruminations about past events and about problems that must be fixed. A mindful attitude recognizes that thoughts are not facts and emotions are not to be avoided. Both are accepted nonjudgmentally as natural parts of life to which a person can choose how to react. This latter idea bears some similarity to Carl Rogers' view that emotional distress is caused by suppressing or distorting emotions to fit what the person has learned should be his or her true feelings and thoughts. Mental health comes with accepting whatever thoughts arise, thus gaining control over them and being able to rationally choose how to respond to them.

Mindfulness involves a concentrated focus on the present and a nonjudgmental acceptance of thoughts and feelings

Mindfulness training, (see, for example, Segal, Williams, & Teasdale, 2002) usually involves a sequence of exercises, such as attending to breathing, as a method of staying in the present, recognizing when the person's mind is wandering into depressive thoughts, disengaging from negative thoughts, recognizing that thoughts are not facts, and keeping a log of these activities in daily life. Continued subclinical depressive thinking after CT predicts relapse and learning and using these mindfulness techniques have been shown to reduce relapse.

4.1.12 Goal Setting

Setting goals and subgoals reorients the person to future life purposes

My Self-Management Therapy program for depression adds several additional components. Goal setting is a treatment component found in a number of programs for self change, such as smoking cessation or dieting programs. As a component strategy for depression, goal setting is based on the idea that people's lives are organized by goals: long-term goals such as career or health goals; medium-sized goals such as running in a 10K race; and short-term goals, such as picking up a gallon of milk on the way home from work. Goals fit together in hierarchies and organize our daily activities. Depressed people are often disconnected from long-term goals. They feel hopeless and helpless about changing their lives, and thus do not pursue distant goals. They may be controlled by the short-term necessities of life. Depressed people also often have long-term goals that are vague or unreachable, again accompanied by helplessness.

The objective of a goal-setting exercise is to orient depressed persons to thinking about longer-term goals and to help them experience success as they pursue these goals. The exercise engages the person in constructive rewarding activity and helps to counter a sense of helplessness. The first step in the exercise is to define a goal. For the purposes of the exercise, it is best to choose an intermediate-term goal, one that can be accomplished in a number of days or weeks. Typical goals involve getting a major job done (cleaning out the garage), socialization (spending more time with others), or self-improvement (starting an exercise or diet program). Rules for a good definition of a goal

Goals should be positive, attainable, concrete, and in the person's control

are borrowed from basic behavior modification principles for defining targets of change. Goals should be (1) *positive*, i.e., something that can be increased in frequency or duration; (2) *attainable*, i.e., something within realistic possibility for the person; (3) *in the person's control*, i.e., within the scope of the person's abilities and efforts, not something controlled by others; and (4) *concrete*, i.e., we should all be able to agree when the goal is accomplished.

Defining a goal is difficult for many depressed people, and it may require discussion and coaching to meet these criteria. Negative goals are common, such as "lose weight" or "quit smoking." These goals are defined by *not* doing something. It is better to define the goal in terms of doing something active and positive, such as "eating healthy meals" or "starting an exercise program."

Unrealistic or perfection goals are also common. "Run a marathon" may or may not be realistic. Often goals are set that invite failure. "Run a mile every day" means that if you miss a day, you have failed. Each day the person runs ought to be a success. "Run a mile at least 4 days a week" might be more realistic. "Find a well-paying job" or "Get married again" may not be within the person's control. "Start a job search" or "start dating again" might be more under the person's control. "Getting healthier" or "Feeling better" are vague goals and it would be difficult to judge whether these goals had been met. "Eating healthier meals" is better because what a healthy meal could be defined concretely.

Subgoals may be sequential steps or related instances of a goal

After a goal is established, subgoals can be written to specify exact behaviors that contribute to the goal. Subgoals could be sequential, as in the steps needed to accomplish the goal, or the subgoals might be various activities that would each contribute to the goal. For example, if the goal was "replace the back fence," subgoals would have to do with removing the old fence, calculating the necessary materials needed, buying the materials, etc. If the goal was to "increase my exercise," subgoals might be things like "take the stairs at work instead of the elevator," "ride my bike to the park on weekends," or " walk to the store instead of drive."

After having some success at one goal, many people develop a second goal as well. Part of the purpose of the exercise with depressed people is to get them to think in terms of goals and planning toward the future, as a kind of reorientation to thinking in terms of longer-term goals.

4.1.13 Self-Reinforcement/Self-Talk

Another component of my Self-Management Program began as an exercise in **Self-Reinforcement**, though we have come to think of it as **Self-Talk**. The self-reinforcement idea derived from the original Self-Control Model of Depression (Rehm, 1977) that posited that depressed people were poor at reinforcing their own goal-directed activities. The original exercise had therapy participants generate some examples of phrases they would comfortably use if complementing or encouraging another person, such as "Good job," "You did that well," or "You are making good progress." Then they are to use these phrases when appropriate to reinforce their own subgoal behavior when working on the goal-setting exercise. When they accomplish a subgoal, they are to say to themselves "I did that well." Or "I am making good progress." In our program, they were also to write these sentences down in their self-monitoring logs as positive self-statements. Although the concept of self-reinforcement still remains somewhat controversial, the exercise can be seen as an attempt to replace the typically negative and discouraging thoughts that depressed people have about their actions with more positive and encouraging thoughts. For many depressed people, the idea of saying anything positive about themselves is bragging or "committing the sin of pride." We point out that if it is alright to congratulate or encourage another person, it should be alright to congratulate or encourage yourself in a realistic way. We would argue that this is what effective people with good self-esteem are doing in their private thoughts. Likewise, bragging occurs when one person is trying to impress another or coerce that person into giving one a compliment. Realistic self-confidence is recognizing when you do something positive and feeling good about it for your own good.

Self-talk is seen as a component of positive self-esteem behavior

4.1.14 Assets List

We have added another component to this, which we refer to as an **Assets List**. As our group participants practice recognizing their own positive activities, we ask them to generalize this experience and describe their own assets. What are your best qualities? What would another person who knew you well say were your best qualities? The exercise is to write down at least five positive qualities. This may not sound like a demanding task, but for depressed people it can sometimes be very difficult, and these clients find it exceptionally difficult to

An Assets List is comprised of the person's positive qualities

> **Clinical Vignette**
> **Confessing Positive Qualities**
>
> In one of our groups, a woman declared that she really could not think of a single positive quality she had. Another group member said, "You were telling me last week about the different kinds of fancy sewing you do. Why don't you write something about that?" After a while she finally wrote, "I am fairly good at some kinds of sewing most of the time." The three qualifiers obviously minimized the value of the positive trait. After some group discussion, this woman was finally convinced that it was acceptable to say "I am good at sewing."

say anything nice about themselves, believing that to do so is bragging and shows a lack of appropriate humility. The Assets List can be very helpful in assisting clients like this to develop a more positive view of themselves.

4.1.15   Other Psychotherapy Components

Emotion focused therapy emphasizes the person's history of emotional experiences and emotion expression and regulation

This list of components is not exhaustive, although I believe they are sufficient to treat most depressions. Other components could be extracted from the different therapy manuals. Emotion-Focused Therapy (Greenberg & Watson, 2005), for example, has a very different rationale. The focus is on the relationship between therapist and client and on the expression of emotion in sessions. It assumes that, through unpleasant experiences of humiliation, loss, and abuse, emotions take on a depressive meaning that involves fears of rejection, judgment, or change, and thus emotion itself is feared. Therapy attempts to increase awareness of emotion and increase emotion regulation, and leads to an ability to reflect on emotion and transform its meaning. The relationship is particularly important as emotional breaches in the therapeutic alliance occur and repairs follow. These situations become especially important learning experiences. It is notable that the expression of emotion is also important in CT, in that only when the person experiences depressive feelings can they experience truly questioning their negative automatic thoughts and crossing the barrier of emotionally biased thinking to retrieve more positive interpretations of experiences.

Short term psychodynamic therapies tend to focus on current problems rather than personality change

A few recent trials of short-term psychodynamic therapies for depression (see, for example, Busch, Rudden, & Shapiro, 2004) have focused on specific current problems rather that personality change and the treatment protocols used in these projects have varied from study to study. An interesting approach that does focus on personality is McCullough's (2000) Cognitive Behavioral Analysis System of Psychotherapy (CBASP). This system is designed to treat chronic depression, and in many ways treats depression as a personality disorder. Recall that Depressive Personality Disorder is in the appendix of the *DSM* as a criterion set provided for further study. CBASP is seen as a lengthy form of psychotherapy aimed at correcting inappropriate relationship habits acquired in childhood.

CBASP is designed to treat chronic depressions in a more extended time frame

Habit change is the goal of Pettit and Joiner's interpersonal approach

In a somewhat similar vein, the therapy manual by Pettit and Joiner (2005) provides a variety of component interventions aimed at altering the habits of depressed persons. Recall that these authors surveyed the literature on how depressed people behave in interpersonal situations as the basis for remedial exercises.

Finally, it is important to note Ellen Frank's (2005) Interpersonal Social Rhythm Therapy. The focus of this therapy is the psychological treatment of bipolar disorder. Based on the idea that bipolar disorder is caused by a dysregulation of circadian rhythms, the therapy encourages strict regularity in daily routines, such as time going to bed and getting up, meal times, etc. Stephen Ilardi (2009) has expanded on this idea as applied to unipolar depression. Ilardi argues that it is the pressures of modern life that have removed us from a healthier past. Improved diet, exercise, and regular routines are among the recommendations he makes for dealing with depression. Circadian rhythms disturbances are also treated by light therapy, as previously discussed.

Regulating circadian rhythms can improve both bipolar and unipolar depressions

4.1.16 Medications

Medications for depression have been described in Chapter 2. For most psychologists and other psychotherapists, the issue becomes when to refer and what considerations should be included in making referral decisions. Clinical lore suggests that medications are more effective for more severe depressions, whereas psychotherapy is more effective for milder depressions. The evidence suggests a more complex picture. Although some studies have found that, among the range of outpatient research volunteers, medications and psychotherapy are equivalent for less severe patients and medications were more effective for severe patients (see, for example, the National Collaborative study; Elkin et al., 1995), an analysis of the combined data from the National Collaborative and three other studies concluded that psychotherapy was equally effective at all levels of severity (DeRubeis, et al. 1999) . It must be remembered, however, that this conclusion is limited to severity among ambulatory volunteer outpatients. As anyone who has worked in an inpatient setting will tell you, there are people who are so severely depressed (e.g., catatonic) or so suicidal that it is almost impossible to carry on a conversation with them, let alone engage them in psychotherapy. Medication or basic behavior modification approaches may be the only possible treatment options for these patients.

Decisions about medication based on severity are complex

Of course, there are people in-between these two extremes. There are depressed persons who are brought in by family members or are coerced to come in. They may be depressed people who have been sitting around the house or refusing to get out of their beds. It may be clear or it may be a judgment call as to whether these people would be helped by an activating antidepressant. Antidepressants can be useful adjuncts to psychotherapy and help people be amenable to psychotherapy at the beginning of the process. Once psychotherapy is well underway, it is often possible to taper people off antidepressants in collaboration with the prescriber.

Another consideration in the decision to medicate is patient preference. Especially in the era of direct advertising to the public by pharmaceutical companies and campaigns aimed at presenting one-dimensional biological views of mental illness, many people will come into treatment believing that they need medication. Years ago I had a conversation with a biological psychiatrist who ran a medication clinic for depression. I was telling him somewhat smugly that I had people coming in to our psychotherapy training clinic saying "I've had tricyclics and I've had SSRIs, now I want the real thing:

The depressed person's preferences are an important factor in treatment

Psychotherapy." He laughed and told me that he saw lots of people who said, "I've had Cognitive Therapy and I've had Interpersonal Therapy, now I want the real thing: Medication." People have their beliefs about what they need and often they seek out referrals to match these beliefs. Some people virtually insist on medications along with psychotherapy. These patients may also require education and persuasion to accept psychotherapy along with medication. For psychotherapy to engage the person, it is import that he or she accept or buy into the rationale for therapy in order for a therapeutic alliance to be formed. Although the research evidence does support a small superiority for the combination of medications and psychotherapy over either modality alone, it also an issue that people may differ in their attributions for progress. Of two people who improve, one may attribute their improvement to the medication and the other to psychotherapy, whatever the therapist might think. It can be important to help people take credit for making the change through their own efforts rather than to passively assume that the medication did it all.

It is important to educate patients about both the positive and negative effects of medications

Therapists typically monitor the positive and negative effects of medications, and it has been documented that there is a wide variation in the information patients have about the medications they are taking. Some prescribers may not tell their patients about the positive effects they should expect. Patients may be disappointed and discontinue early if they are not told how long it may take for the medication to have an effect. They might experience an increase in energy and not attribute it to the medication. On the other hand, some prescribers do not cover very thoroughly the potential side effects that patients may experience, and unexpected side effects may lead patients to discontinue their medications, even when they are having a positive effect. Psychotherapists share responsibility with the prescriber for monitoring these effects.

4.2   Mechanisms of Action

Increasing rewarding behavior is one of the basic mechanisms of action underlying behavioral and interpersonal theories

The mechanisms of action for the behavioral and cognitive therapies are not well established. Behavior therapy, behavioral activation, and the interpersonal- and social-skill approaches share an assumption that depression involves a deficiency in functional reward for positive behavior. Lewinsohn (1974) defines this as "a loss or lack of response contingent positive reinforcement." Others are less explicit, but the assumption of the skill models is that the person is deficient in skills and thus is not obtaining life's rewards to the extent necessary to maintain positive behavior, a positive outlook, and positive mood.

Increasing positive, pleasurable, and functional behavior per se is one mechanism for influencing mood. Skill approaches are designed to teach functional and interpersonal skills that will lead to greater pleasure and satisfaction in interaction with others. There is an assumption that, as the person becomes more active, natural reinforcers will maintain the behaviors that were lost during the episode of depression. An interesting additional assumption is that depressive behavior may be reinforced in the form of sympathy from those in the depressed person's social network, but that the depressive behavior is aversive in the long run and actually functions to turn people away and reduce reinforcement. There is also an implicit assumption that there are ratios of behavior to reinforcement that are sufficient to maintain euthymic behavior and there are ratios that are insufficient and will lead to depression. Some people who are very active may nonetheless be depressed because the amount of effort is disproportional to the amount of reinforcement received. Similarly, some people who are relatively inactive may still receive high levels of reinforcement and remain quite happy.

A substantial number of studies have tracked activity level and mood, and simply enhancing activity levels may be one of the core mechanisms for change. Measurement often consists of simple self-monitoring, but more objective measures such as mechanical activity monitors or observers have been used, and various mood scales and questionnaires have been used to assess level of depressive symptoms. Both pleasure and mastery events are usually recorded. In general, positive activities and events, whether contingent or not, correlate with positive mood, and negative activities and events, whether contingent or not, correlate with negative mood. In a few therapy outcome studies, increases in activity correlate with increases in mood across participants.

Mood has been demonstrated to vary as a function of positive and negative activities

The cognitive metaphor stresses that feelings are based on our interpretation of events and that these interpretations can be erroneous, distorted, or biased. In depression, people's interpretations of events are negative, leading to depressed mood. The negative interpretations reflected a changed perception of the world based on a filter acquired from negative experiences in childhood. Beck's cognitive approach assumes that these early acquired schemas may become latent and are reactivated by negative events in adulthood. This suggests an all-or-none mechanism in which the negative schema is either latent or active. An alternative view described by Rehm and Naus (1990) is that life events, their interpretations, and the generalizations that are derived from them have a valence from sad to happy. A person's current mood facilitates access to memories and interpretations of events that have a similar valence. This type of account allows for degrees of sadness and happiness, and degrees of negative or positive interpretations. In either case, as a person remains depressed, these selective memories strengthen the negative system of interpretations. In the natural course of events, the depressed person may become less depressed if he or she encounters positive events that restore access to positive interpretations. In such cases, the overall structure of negative and positive associations remains unaltered. Current mood simply maintains access to a subset of possible interpretations of events. A person's susceptibility to depression remains if he or she has a subset of interpretations that are strongly negatively valenced and are thus easily accessed when another negative life event occurs.

Changing negative distortions of events is a second theoretical basic mechanism of action

Mood influences whether the person interprets an event positively or negatively

Therapy from the cognitive point of view involves helping the person to correct his or her negative distortions by considering alternative interpretations and logically or empirically testing the validity of each interpretation. These clients must learn to overcome their automatic thoughts that have been facilitated by a negative mood and access an interpretation that does not have a negative valence. Thus, the overall mechanism of change is first to learn to counter initial negative biases in thinking by questioning them and searching for more positive interpretations, and, it is hoped, in doing so they will reconstruct interpretive schemas so that this tendency will no longer direct interpretations to negative possibilities.

There have been a number of efforts to validate the idea that changes in schemas mediate changes in depression in CT. For example, in one study it was found that change from pretreatment to midtreatment on measures of depressive cognition predicted changes in depressive symptoms from midtreatment to posttreatment for participants in CT, but not for those in a medication condition (DeRubeis, et al., 1990). Although not all studies have produced such clear results, there is support for the mediation role of cognitive change in CT.

Countering helplessness is a third theoretical mechanism of action

The third primary metaphor for the nature of depression is the helplessness/hopelessness model. When people make internal, stable, and general attributions for a major negative event in their lives, they may conclude that they are helpless to prevent such events happening again, and this generalization may lead to hopelessness about the future and to depression. Note that behavioral activation and skill training may restore a sense of efficacy by showing the person that he or she can do things effectively, and changing negative interpretations of an event may change negative attributions as a path to overcoming helplessness. In outcome studies of different therapies, helpless has been reduced as an outcome measure.

4.3   Efficacy and Prognosis

4.3.1   Efficacy

Research evaluating the outcome of psychotherapy for depression began in the 1970s

Outcome studies evaluating the efficacy of psychotherapy for depression did not begin until the early 1970s. In 1973, two small studies were published: Shipley and Fazio (1973) evaluated a problem-solving therapy with mildly depressed college students, and McLean, Ogston, and Grauer (1973) assessed an eclectic set of behavioral modules from which therapists were allowed to choose, based on the particular client. Even at this starting point, fairly complex packages of therapy with multiple components were being evaluated. Very little research has focused on evaluating components per se.

Most studies evaluate complex therapy packages; only a few have evaluated components of therapy

In a study of the components of Lewinsohn's behavior therapy, Zeiss, Lewinsohn, and Munoz (1979) compared the efficacy of interpersonal skills training, pleasant activity schedules, and cognitive training. They found no differences in outcome regardless of whether or not the measure matched the treatment. A few studies have studied components in dismantling strategies (Jacobson et al., 1996; Rehm et al., 1981), but as discussed elsewhere, it is hard to evaluate components added on to one another. Arthur Nezu (1986) did an evaluation of Problem Solving Therapy (Nezu, Nezu, & Perri, 1989) and demonstrated its efficacy for depression. Although it, too, is something of a package program, it is about the closest to a single treatment component being assessed. Recently, a review of 34 studies representing four different approaches to Behavioral Activation (Mazzucchelli, Kane, & Rees, 2009) found them to be effective and equal overall to the effectiveness of CT.

My review of efficacy research focuses on the progress that has been made on evaluating treatment packages overall, and I try to look at overall trends in the research rather than evaluation of specific components or packages.

The late 1960s and early 1970s was an era when new models of depression were being proposed. Basic research on the models began in some instances, but in most cases the models were developed as a basis for designing interventions. These interventions were assessed first in validation studies in which they were tested against control conditions, primarily waiting lists, no treatment, or some form of placebo therapy.

Manuals were published to standardize the therapies and to allow others to apply and assess them. Among these were Peter Lewinsohn's Behavior Therapy (1974), Aaron Beck's CT (1963; Beck, Rush, Shaw, & Emery, 1979), my Self-Control/Self-Management Therapy (Rehm, 1977), and Gerald Klerman and Myrna Weissman's IPT (Klerman, Weissman, Rounsaville, & Chevron, 1984). Other models, such as Seligman's helplessness model (Abramson, Seligman, & Teasdale, 1978), and treatments, such as Nezu's Problem Solving treatment (Nezu, Nezu, & Perri, 1989), followed.

Many treatment manuals with very different rationales were tested and validated during this era. All were demonstrated to be better than no treatment controls, and in most trials they also were better than placebo controls. In general, psychotherapies for depression are better than no-treatment control conditions.

The next era of research during the 1980s tended to compare one psychotherapy against another. Comparisons between representative cognitive and behavioral therapies were common. Several reviews during this era concluded that there were no differences between different psychotherapies (Rehm & Kaslow, 1984).

Comparisons and combinations with medications for depression followed. Prominent among these studies was the National Collaborative study (Elkin, Shea, Watkins, & Imber, 1989). This study had several novel features. Because medications have been evaluated many more times than psychotherapies, both a medication and placebo medication condition were employed in the study. Each was used as a gauge for assessing the comparison psychotherapies, Beck's CT and Klerman and Weissman's IPT. Four sites administered the protocol. Not only the psychotherapies, but the medication and placebo administration were also manualized to assure standard procedures. The study was an attempt to move psychotherapy research out of a situation in which many small studies led to inconclusive results to a norm of larger studies yielding more definitive results. In the study, 239 depressed patients were treated for 16 weeks.

CT and IPT were shown to be equally effective in treating depression compared to the reference medication. There was limited evidence of the effectiveness of interpersonal, but not CT, when compared with the placebo condition. There was also evidence of the superiority of both psychotherapies over placebo in the recovery analysis. The standardized medication clinical management led to an unusually strong placebo effect in this study.

Among the studies evaluating the combination of medication and psychotherapy, a study by Keller and colleagues stands out (Keller et al., 2000). This huge study with 681 participants compared the medication nefazodone to McCullough's therapy for chronic depression and their combination. The results demonstrated independent effects for each of the treatments and an additive effect for their combination.

In the 1960s and 1970s, models of depression were proposed, manuals were developed, and initial evaluation studies were begun

In the 1980s research began to focus on comparisons between psychotherapies

Psychotherapy compared to and combined with medication was the next trend in outcome research

Most forms of psychotherapy are equally effective

Research finds medications equally effective in comparison to one another and in comparison with psychotherapy

The combination of psychotherapy and medication is slightly superior to either alone

In general, the results of these comparison and combination studies reveal no differences in the effectiveness of different psychotherapies for depression. A recent report of a series of meta-analyses of outcome studies for depression found a slight advantage for IPT and a disadvantage for nondirective supportive treatment, but concluded that the effect was so small that treatments were essentially equivalent to one another (Cuijpers, van Straten, Andersson, & van Oppen, 2008). It is important to note that studies of different medications for depression, even when comparing the older tricyclics with the newer SSRIs and SNRIs, similarly find no differences among medications. The only differences are in side-effect profiles. It may not be surprising then that no differences exist in the effectiveness of psychotherapies and mediations for depression when they are compared with one another (Agency for Health Care Policy and Research, 1993). Although it has not been a consistent finding, *most studies suggest the combination of medication and psychotherapy is slightly superior to either alone* (Conte, Plutchik, Wild, & Karasu, 1986).

4.3.2   Prognosis and Relapse

Depression is a chronic disorder

Depression is a chronic disorder. According to the *DSM* (American Psychiatric Association, 2000), after a first episode of depression the likelihood of a second episode if 50%, and after a second episode the likelihood of a third is 70%. One parameter of effective intervention is the ability to prevent or reduce relapse.

Psychotherapy appears superior to medication in preventing relapse

In the medication literature, relapse prevention is largely a matter of medication continuation into maintenance phases which may be quite lengthy. Comparisons between psychotherapy and medication demonstrate that psychotherapy is superior in preventing relapse, even in comparison to continuation medication (Vittengl, Clark, Dunn, & Jarrett, 2007). Continuation cognitive behavior therapy further reduces relapse rates. It should be noted that these studies are largely studies of Beck's CT and IPT, which have been the most extensively studied forms of therapy in research evaluating the relative efficacy of psychotherapy and medication.

4.4   Variations and Combinations of Treatments

4.4.1   Applications to Different Populations

One of the frequent criticisms of manualized therapies is that they are rigid and designed to be "one size fits all." In general, this is an over simplification. The manuals that I have reviewed all address the individual and unique problems of particular people. They may do so with a particular language and with a particular set of strategies, but these strategies are always adapted to the individual client.

Psychotherapies have been adapted for different phases of the life span, but research is limited

Adapting treatment for different populations is a continuing issue for psychotherapies for depression. Adaptations have been made for different age groups for many of the therapies. A number of studies have been done demonstrating effectiveness with elderly populations (see, for example, Rokke, Tomhave, & Jocic, 1999 and Thompson, Gallagher, & Breckenridge, 1987), and manuals for Behavioral Therapy, CT, and IPT have been published for the elderly (see Chapter 5). Treatments for depression in children and adolescents have also been adapted from the adult treatments. This literature has been reviewed by Kaslow, McClure, and Connell (2002) and by Lewinsohn and Clarke (1999). Manuals for therapy with adolescents have been developed for Behavior Therapy by Lewinsohn and his colleagues, for IPT, and for an eclectic therapy by Stark and colleagues (see Chapter 5).

4.4.2   Treatment Formats

Although most of the treatments described above are typically delivered in individual therapy format, group, family, and marital formats have also been reported. My Self-Management Therapy program has always been employed for research purposes in a group format, although the program sometimes is used in an individual format with depressed people in our training clinic. Peter Lewinsohn offers his Behavioral program in a classroom format, *The Coping with Depression Course* (Lewinsohn, Antonuccio, Steinmetz-Breckenridge, & Teri, 1984). Other therapies, such as CT, have been adapted to a group format (Yost, Beutler, Corbishley, & Allender, 1986) . Family therapy has also been used for treating depression, especially in children and adolescents (Kaslow & Racusin, 1994). The rationale for family therapy is that depression is an interpersonal phenomenon, and in families it may also be parental depression that is influencing child and adolescent depression. Marital therapy has also been employed in the treatment of depression (Beach, Sandeen, & O'Leary, 1990) based on the same rationale. Also there has been a great deal of research on depression and marital interactions. Depressed spouses coerce nondepressed spouses into giving in to them, and nondepressed spouses may inadvertently reinforce depression in their spouses.

Depression has been treated in individual, group, family, and marital formats

4.4.3   Sequencing with Medication

In the medication literature, treatment strategies are described for dealing with initial treatment nonresponse or partial response, using augmentation or alternative medications. Would medication nonresponders respond to psychotherapy and vice versa? Some beginning answers to these questions have been provided by a large study of sequenced treatments, the STAR*D project (Thase et al., 2007). When participants failed to respond to an initial trial of medication in this study, they were switched to an alternative or augmented treatment. CT as a second-step alternative did as well as augmented medication or an alternative medication. We are likely to learn more from future studies about individual differences in response to different treatments and treatment modalities that will allow for matching of treatment to the individual characteristics.

Sequencing psychotherapy and medication has only recently begun to be studied systematically

4.5   Problems in Carrying Out the Treatments

Most psychotherapies for depression involve homework, and compliance is an issue

Nearly all of the therapies and therapy components rely on homework assignments, and homework compliance is a frequent problem in treating depression. Indeed, lethargy and difficulty in carrying out tasks is a symptom of depression. "Can you really expect a depressed person to do homework?" is a question I am frequently asked in treatment workshops. "Yes, you can" is the answer, but under the right circumstances. First, it is important to make homework assignments practical. "Keep them simple" is a fundamental rule. In our group format program, we want people to monitor positive activities and mood on a daily basis as a basic assignment. However, for the first week we ask participants to monitor mood only. Participants rate their average mood for the day on a simple 0 to 10 scale: 0 is the worst day you ever had and 10 is the best day. To keep the process simple, we do not use any other anchors. The first-day rating is used as a standard for the second day, and we ask patients to note variations in mood. Mood obviously varies throughout the day, and some research studies have had people monitor their mood throughout the day. However, we find that a simple single rating is quite sufficient for noting daily ups and downs of mood. Similarly, when we ask people to monitor positive events we recognize that some events are of much greater magnitude than others and have a much greater influence on mood. Weighting event magnitude increases the correlation with mood, but a simple total number of events is sufficient to demonstrate a relationship.

Another strategy that is often helpful in getting people to do homework assignments is to construe them as experiments. They are not guaranteed cures, they may sound trivial, they may seem unlikely to have any real effect, but as experiments they are worth giving a try to see if the individual person does learn something, experience a change, or see his or her situation in a different way.

Several of the therapy manuals address the fact that it is important that the client accept the rationale for the treatment. Indeed, *establishing an agreed-upon view of the problem and an agreed-upon approach to dealing with it is the basis for an effective therapeutic alliance.* People often come into treatment with views of their problems that may not fit our therapy models. "I read that depression is all brain chemistry" or "It was my parents that messed me up" are initial attitudes that do not mesh well with most cognitive-behavioral treatments. Education and persuasion may be necessary for the depressed person to understand and accept the therapy rationale. These therapies are transparent, so describing and discussing the underlying model and rationale for treatment can be very helpful to establishing a collaborative approach to dealing with the problem. In addition, it is often necessary to show the person how this approach applies to their individual situation. Another attitude assumed by some people is "My problems are unique and no one can really understand them."

Aaron Beck et al. (1979) describe an interesting approach to encouraging homework compliance. At the end of the first session in which the therapist gives the person a homework assignment and gets the person's agreement that the assignment is worth trying, the therapist then gives the person an inventory of "reasons for not doing homework," devised by Beck and his colleague, David Burns. The person checks off any reasons that they might have for not doing homework, and the therapist then discusses with them how they might overcome this barrier. For example, if clients indicates that they really do not have time for homework, the therapist works with them to find ways to schedule the homework activity.

The ultimate problem in carrying out treatment is what to do when the treatment is not working. First, it is important to acknowledge the problem and discuss it with the person in treatment. Sometime people admit that they do not think that the therapy is addressing some problem that they think is more important, but have not brought up or have downplayed. Prioritizing problems and choosing appropriate treatment components to address top priorities may help restore therapeutic momentum.

It is also important to assess whether the therapist's characteristics and general approach are a match to the person's personality and whether the lack of a match might be hampering progress in therapy. Beutler, Clarkin, and Bongar's (2000) principles identifying effective relationship, treatment, client, and therapist factors may be useful in these situations.

4.6   Multicultural Issues

Culture, race, and ethnicity pose challenges to the applicability of our treatments for depression. A report of the US Surgeon General (US Department of Health and Human Services, 2001) cites problems in availability of and access to services by minority individuals. Higher rates of poverty, unemployment, lack of health insurance, unfamiliarity, and mistrust may also contribute to underutilization and paucity of quality services. Minority populations in the US are clearly underserved.

Despite three and a half decades of efficacy research we are only beginning to see trials with sufficient minority representation to assess the applicability of our treatment to minority groups. Two core questions remain unanswered. Are adaptations of treatments necessary for them to be applied with minority individuals? Do the treatments need to be delivered in a different way for members of minority groups?

If individuals come from groups that are more family and community centered, it may be helpful to include the extended family and even religious leaders in the treatment process. Evidence is accumulating for outcomes of treatment with minority populations, and this literature suggests that current validated treatments can be effectively applied to various minority groups, albeit sometimes with cultural adaptations (Griner & Smith, 2006). Clearly, more research is needed to firmly establish the cultural generalizabilty of treatments and culture-specific adaptations.

Research on psychotherapy for depression in different cultural, racial, and ethnic groups is in an early stage, but results suggest that psychotherapy is effective with almost all populations

5

Further Reading

What follows in this chapter is a list of therapy manuals and patient workbooks for treating depression. Most are published, readily available, and written in a way that allows the therapist to administer the particular therapy without additional training. Many were developed in the course of research that evaluated the treatment. Workbooks for therapy or research participants can often serve as self-help books as well.

Behavior Therapy

Lewinsohn, P. M., Antonuccio, D. O., Steinmetz-Breckenridge, J. L., & Teri, L. (1984). *The coping with depression course: A psychoeducational intervention for unipolar depression.* Eugene, OR: Castalia Publishing.
Version of Lewinsohn's program suitable for presentation as an educational classroom program.

Brown, M. A., & Lewinsohn, P. M. (1984). *Participant workbook for the coping with depression course.* Eugene, OR: Castalia Publishing.
The workbook for the classroom can also serve as a self-help book and has been found to achieve equivalent results.

Lewinsohn, P. M., Munoz, R. F., Youngren, M. A., & Zeiss, A. M. (1986). *Control your depression* (2nd ed.). Englewood Cliffs, NJ: Prentice-Hall.
More detailed self-help version of the program.

Martell, C. R., Addis, M. E., & Jacobson, N. S. (2002). *Depression in context: Strategies for guided action.* New York: W. W. Norton.
Behavioral activation is the central content of this book, with additional strategies.

McCullough, J. P. (2000). *Treatment for chronic depression: Cognitive behavioral analysis system of psychotherapy.* New York: Guilford Press.
Chronic depression includes dysthymia and extended MDD. Depression here is treated almost like a personality disorder.

Cognitive Therapy

Beck, A. T., Rush, A. J., Shaw, B., & Emery, G. (1979). *Cognitive therapy of depression.* New York: Guilford Press.
Most of the studies of cognitive therapy are based on this manual.

Beck, J. S. (1995). *Cognitive therapy: Basics and beyond.* New York: Guilford Press.
The author is Aaron Beck's daughter, Judith, and the book is an update of the therapy manual with many bells and whistles.

Persons, J. B., Davidson, J., & Tompkins, M. A. (2001). *Essential components of cognitive-behavior therapy for depression.* Washington, DC: American Psychological Association.
An excellent beginner's book for graduate students or for a therapist who wants to teach him or herself the basics of cognitive therapy. I have used it in practicum for several years.

Zettle, R. D. (2007). *ACT for depression: A clinician's guide to using acceptance and commitment therapy in treating depression*. Oakland, CA: New Harbinger Press.

ACT attempts to increase the person's flexibility in responding in a variety of contexts which are associated with depression. Multiple techniques are used: some common, some unique.

Rehm, L. P. (2005). *Self-management therapy for depression*. Unpublished manuscript, University of Houston.

My structured group manual is available at LPRehm@uh.edu.

Interpersonal Pychotherapies

Klerman, G. L., Weissman, M. M., Rounceville, B. J., & Chevron, E. S. (1984). *Interpersonal psychotherapy for depression*. New York: Basic Books.

The initial therapy manual based on the early studies of this therapy.

Weissman, M. M. (2000). *Mastering depression through interpersonal psychotherapy*. New York: Elsevier Science and Technology Books.

An updated therapy manual used for more recent research studies.

Weissman, M. M., Markowitz, J. C., & Klerman, G. L. (2007). *A clinician's guide to interpersonal psychotherapy*. New York: Oxford Press.

A practical guide for therapists to learn IPT.

Pettit, J. W., & Joiner, T. E. (2005). The interpersonal solution to depression: A workbook for changing how you feel by changing how you relate. Oakland, CA: New Harbinger Publications.

This workbook describes a number of innovative interventions that are derived from research on the behavior of depressed people in interpersonal relationship,

Becker, R. E., Heimberg, R., & Bellack, A. (1987). *Social skills training treatment for depression*. New York: Pergamon.

This was the therapy manual for a large study of social-skills treatment for depression.

Nezu, A. M., Nezu, C. M., & Perri, M. G. (1989). *Problem solving therapy for depression: Theory, research and clinical guidelines*. New York: Wiley.

Rationale, research review, and problem-solving interventions for depression.

Beach, S. R. H., Sandeen, E. E., & O'Leary, K. D. (1990). *Depression in marriage: A model for etiology and treatment*. New York: Guilford Press.

A behavioral marital therapy approach to therapy for depressed spouses.

Emotion and Psychodynamic Therapies

Greenberg, L., & Watson, J. (2005). *Emotion focused therapy for depression*. Washington, DC: American Psychological Association.

Emotions (fears of rejection, change, feelings, etc.) are analyzed in a broad context of meaning. Therapy increases emotional awareness and regulation, allowing clients to reflect on and transform emotion.

Busch, F. N., Rudden, M., & Shapiro, T. (2004). *Psychodynamic treatment of depression*. Washington, DC: American Psychiatric Publications.

A focused form of psychodynamic therapy based on a particular formulation. A number of specific problems in treating depression are addressed.

Treatment Decision Making

Beutler, L. E., Clarkin, J. F., & Bongar, B. (2000). *Guidelines for the systematic treatment of the depressed patient*. New York: Oxford University Press.

Guidelines abstracted from the psychotherapy literature for relationship, treatment, client, and therapist factors as they apply to depression.

Parker, G., & Manicavasagar, V. (2005). *Modeling and managing the depressive disorders: A clinical guide*. Cambridge, UK: Cambridge University Press.

An alternative view of classification of depressions and treatment recommendations for various types based on diagnosis and on basic personality traits.

Children and Adolescents

Clarke, G. N., Lewinsohn, P. M., & Hops, H. (1990). Adolescent coping with depression course. Eugene, OR: Castalia Publishing.

Lewinsohn, P. M., & Hops, H. (1990). *Adolescents coping with depression course/Student workbook*. Eugene, OR: Castalia Publishing.

Lewinsohn, P. M., Rhode, P., Hops, H., & Clarke, G. N. (1991). *Adolescent coping with depression course: Leader's manual for parent groups*. Eugene, OR: Castalia Publishing.

Lewinsohn, P. M., Rohde, P., Clarke, G. N., & Hops, H. (1991). Adolescent coping with depression course: Parent workbook. Eugene, OR: Castalia Publishing.

These four books relate to a program for use in high schools and may or may not include a parental component.

Mufson, L., Dorta, K., Moreau, D., & Weissman, M. M. (2004). *Interpersonal psychotherapy for depressed adolescents*. (2nd ed.). New York: Guilford Press.

IPT adapted for use with adolescents.

Stark, K. D. (1990). *Childhood depression: School based intervention*. New York: Guilford Press.

An eclectic set of strategies for use in the classroom and in counseling depressed children in schools.

Stark, K., & Kendall, P. C. (1996). *Treating depressed children: Therapist manual for "Taking Action."* Ardmore, PA: Workbook Publishing.

Stark, K., Kendall, P. C., McCarthy, M., Stafford, M., Barron, R., & Thomeer, M. (1996). *Taking action: A workbook for overcoming depression* [Client Workbook]. Ardmore, PA: Workbook Publishing.

An updated and more systematic program using many of the same strategies as in the earlier book. Illustrated with cartoons.

The Elderly

Yost, E. B., Beutler, L. E., Corbishley, M. A., & Allender, J. R. (1986). *Group cognitive therapy: A treatment approach for depressed older adults.* New York: Pergamon Books.

CT adapted for the elderly and for group administration.

Gallagher, D., & Thompson, L. W. (2010). *Treating late life depression: A cognitive-behavioral therapy approach, therapist guide.* New York: Oxford University Press

Thompson, L. W., Dick-Siskin, L., Coon, D. W., Powers, D. V., & Gallagher, D. (2009). *Treating late life depression: A cognitive-behavioral therapy approach, workbook (treatments that work).* New York: Oxford University Press

An updated program combining cognitive therapy, behavior therapy, emotion focus, and some interpersonal communication strategies.

Hinrichsen, G. A., & Clougherty, K. F. (2006). *Interpersonal psychotherapy for depressed older adults.* Washington, DC: American Psychological Association.

IPT adapted.

Qualls, S. H., & Knight, B. G. (2006). *Psychotherapy for depression in older adults.* New York: Wiley.

Describes how to use behavior therapy, interpersonal therapy, and cognitive therapy adapted for older adults in a variety of settings.

Bipolar disorder

Frank, E. (2005). *Treating bipolar disorder: A clinician's guide to interpersonal and social rhythm therapy.* New York: Guilford Press.

IPT combined with strategies for regularizing daily routines to smooth out biological rhythms.

Basco, M. R., & Rush, A. J. (2005). *Cognitive behavior therapy for bipolar disorder* (2nd ed.). New York: Guilford Press.

Basco, M. R. (2006). *The bipolar workbook: Tools for controlling your mood swings.* New York: Guilford Press.

A variety of cognitive-behavioral strategies plus medication in an overall management program for dealing with bipolar disorder in its many phases.

Reiser, R. P., & Thompson, L. W. (2005). *Bipolar disorder.* New York: Hogrefe & Huber.

Practical recommendations for diagnoses and treatment of depression based on empirically supported techniques.

6

References

Abraham, K. (1911). Notes on the psychoanalytic investigation and treatment of manic-depressive insanity and allied conditions. In *Selected papers of Karl Abraham* (pp. 137–156). London: Hogarth.

Abramson, L. Y., Metalsky, G. I., & Alloy, L. B. (1989). Hopelessness depression: A theory-based subtype of depression. *Psychological Review*, *96*, 358–372.

Abramson, L. Y., Seligman, M. E. P., & Teasdale, J. (1978). Learned helplessness in humans: Critique and reformulation. *Journal of Abnormal Psychology*, *87*, 49–74.

Agency for Health Care Policy and Research. (1993). *Depression in primary care. Vol. 2, Treatment of major depression*. Rockville, MD: US Department of Health and Human Services, Public Health Service, Agency for Health Care Policy and Research.

American Psychiatric Association. (2000). *Diagnostic and statistical manual of mental disorders* (4th ed.). Washington, DC: APA

Anderson, C. B., Rehm, L. P., & Mehta, P. (2003). The revised self-control questionnaire for depression: Psychometric properties and relation to depression. Unpublished manuscript, University of Houston.

Arieti, S., & Bemporad, J. R. (1980). The psychological organization of depression. *American Journal of Psychiatry*, *137*, 1360–1365.

Barber, J. P., & Muenz, L. R. (1996). The role of avoidance and obsessiveness in matching patients to cognitive and interpersonal psychotherapy. *Journal of Consulting and Clinical Psychology*, *64*, 951–958.

Beach, S. R. H., Sandeen, E. E., & O'Leary, K. D. (1990). *Depression in marriage: A model for etiology and treatment*. New York: Guilford Press.

Beck, A. T. (1963). Thinking and depression. *Archives of General Psychiatry*, *9*, 324–333.

Beck, A. T. (1972). *Depression: Causes and treatment*. Philadelphia: University of Pennsylvania Press.

Beck, A. T. (1983). Cognitive therapy of depression: New perspectives. In P. J. Clayton & J. E. Barnett (Eds.), *Treatment of depression: Old controversies and new approaches* (pp. 265–290). New York: Raven Press.

Beck, A. T., Rush, A. J., Shaw, B. F., & Emery, G. (1979). *Cognitive therapy for depression*. New York: Guilford Press.

Beck, A. T., Steer, R. A., & Brown, G. K. (1996). *Manual for the BDI-II*. San Antonio, TX: The Psychological Corporation.

Beck, A. T., Steer, R. A., & Garbin, M. G. (1988). Psychometric properties of the Beck Depression Inventory: Twenty-five years of evaluation. *Clinical Psychology Review*, *8*, 77–100.

Beck, A. T., Ward, C. H., Mendelsohn, M., Mock, J., & Erbaugh, J. (1961). An inventory for measuring depression. *Archives of General Psychiatry*, *4*, 561–571.

Bellack, A. S., Hersen, M., & Himmelhoch, J. (1981). Social skills training compared with pharmacotherapy and psychotherapy in the treatment of unipolar depression. *American Journal of Psychiatry*, *138*, 1562–1567.

Beutler, L. E., Castonguay, L. C., & Follette, W. C. (2006). Integration of therapeutic factors in dysphoric disorders. In L. C. Castonguay & L. E. Beutler (Eds.), *Principles of therapeutic change that work: Integrating relationship, treatment, client and therapist variables* (pp. 111–117). New York: Oxford University Press.

Beutler, L. E., Clarkin, J. F., & Bongar, B. (2000). *Guidelines for the systematic treatment of the depressed patient.* New York: Oxford University Press.

Bieling, P. J., Beck, A. T., & Brown, G. K. (2000). The sociotropy-autonomy scale: Structure and implications. *Cognitive Therapy & Research, 24,* 763–779.

Blatt, S. J., Quinlan, D. M., Chevron, E. S., McDonald, C., & Zuroff, D. (1982). Dependency and self-criticism: Psychological dimensions of depression. *Journal of Consulting and Clinical Psychology, 50,* 113–124.

Blatt, S. J., Quinlan, D. M., Pilkonis, P. A., & Shea, M. T. (1995). Impact of perfectionism and need for approval on the brief treatment of depression: The National Institute of Mental Health Treatment of Depression Collaborative Research Program revisited. *Journal of Consulting and Clinical Psychology, 63,* 125–132.

Brommelhoff, J. A., Conway, K., Merikangas, K. R., & Levy, B. R. (2004). Higher rates of depression in women: Role of gender bias with the family. *Journal of Women's Health, 13,* 69–76.

Brown, G. W., & Harris, T. (1984). *Social origins of depression: A study of psychiatric disorder in women.* London: Tavistock Publishers.

Burns, D. D. (1999). *Feeling good: The new mood therapy* (revised and updated ed.). New York: Avon.

Busch, F. N., Rudden, M., & Shapiro, T. (2004). *Psychodynamic treatment of depression.* Washington, DC: American Psychiatric Publications.

Butcher, J. N., Dahlstrom, W. G., Graham, J. R., Tellegen, A., & Kraemmer, B. (1989). *The Minnesota Multiphasic Personality Inventory - 2 (MMPI-2): Manual for the administration and scoring.* Minneapolis, MN: University of Minnesota Press.

Cantor, N., Smith, E. E., French, R., & Mezzich, J. (1980). Psychiatric diagnosis as prototype categorization. *Journal of Abnormal Psychology, 89,* 181–193

Carroll, B. J. (1998). *Carroll Depression Scales-Revised (CDS-R): Technical manual.* Toronto: Multi-Health Systems.

Carroll, B. J., Feinberg, M., Smouse, P. E., Rawson, S. G., & Greden, J. F. (1981). The Carroll Rating Scale for Depression: I. Development, reliability, and validation. *British Journal of Psychiatry, 138,* 194–200.

Castonguay, L. C., & Beutler, L. E. (Eds.). (2006). *Principles of therapeutic change that work: Integrating relationship, treatment, client and therapist variables.* New York: Oxford University Press.

Centers for Disease Control and Prevention. (2008). Prevalence of self-reported postpartum depressive symptoms--17 states, 2004–2005. *The Journal of the American Medical Association, 299,* 2268–2270.

Chambers, W. J., Puig-Antich, J., Hirsch, M., Paez, P., Ambrosini, P. J., Tabrizi, M. A., et al. (1985). The assessment of affective disorders in children and adolescents by semi-structured interview. Test-retest reliability of the schedule for affective disorders and schizophrenia for school-age children, present episode version. *Archives of General Psychiatry, 42,* 696–702.

Clark, L. A., & Watson, D. (1991). Tripartite model of anxiety and depression: Psychometric evidence and taxonomic implications. *Journal of Abnormal Psychology, 100,* 316–336.

Conte, H. R., Plutchik, R., Wild, K. V., & Karasu, T. B. (1986). Combined psychotherapy and pharmacotherapy for depression: A systematic analysis of the evidence. *Archives of General Psychiatry, 43,* 471–479.

Coyne, J. C. (1976). Depression and the response of others. *Journal of Abnormal Psychology, 85,* 186–193.

Cross-National Collaborative Group. (1992). The changing rate of major depression. Cross-national comparisons. *The Journal of the American Medical Association, 268,* 3098–3105.

Cuijpers, P., van Straten, A., Andersson, G., & van Oppen, P. (2008). Psychotherapy for depression in adults: A meta-analysis of comparative outcome studies. *Journal of Consulting and Clinical Psychology, 76,* 909–922.

Cyranowski, J., Frank, E., Young, E., & Shear, K. (2000). Adolescent onset of the gender difference in lifetime rates of major depression: A theoretical model. *Archives of General Psychiatry, 57,* 21–27.

Dempsey, P. (1964). A multidimensional depression scale for the MMPI. *Journal of Counseling Psychology, 28*, 364–370.

DeRubeis, R. J., Evans, M. D., Hollon, S. D., Garvey, M. J., Grove, W. M., & Tuason, V. B. (1990). How does cognitive therapy work? Cognitive change and symptom change in cognitive therapy and pharmacotherapy for depression. *Journal of Consulting and Clinical Psychology, 58*, 862–869.

DeRubeis, R. J., Gelfand, L. A., Tang, T. Z., & Simons, A. D. (1999). Medications versus cognitive behavior therapy for severely depressed outpatients: mega-analysis of four randomized comparisons. *American Journal of Psychiatry, 156*, 1007–1013.

Dozois, D. J. A., Dobson, K. S., & Ahnberg, J. L. (1998). A psychometric evaluation of the Beck Depression Inventory-II. *Psychological Assessment, 10*, 83–89.

Eaton, W. W., Anthony, J. C., Gallo, J., Cai, G., Tien, A., Romanoski, A., et al. (1997). Natural history of Diagnostic Interview Schedule/DSM-IV major depression: The Baltimore epidemiologic catchment area follow-up. *Archives of General Psychiatry, 54*, 993–999.

Ekman, P., & Friesen, W. V. (1974). Non-verbal behavior in psychopathology. In R. J. Friedman & M. M. Katz (Eds.), *The psychology of depression: Contemporary theory and research* (pp. 203–224). New York: Winston-Wiley.

Elkin, I., Gibbons, R. D., Shea, M. T., Sotsky, S. M., Watkins, J. T., Pilkonis, P. A., et al. (1995). Initial severity and differential treatment outcome in the National Institute of Mental Health Treatment of Depression Collaborative Research Program. *Journal of Consulting and Clinical Psychology, 63*, 841–847.

Elkin, I., Shea, M. T., Watkins, J. T., & Imber, S. D. (1989). National Institute of Mental Health Treatment of Depression Collaborative Research Program: General effectiveness of treatments. *Archives of General Psychiatry, 46*, 971–982.

Feighner, J. P., Robins, E., Guze, S., Woodruff, R. A., Winokur, G., & Munoz, R. (1972). Diagnostic criteria for use in psychiatric research. *Archives of General Psychiatry, 26*, 57–63.

First, M. B., Spitzer, R. L., Gibbon, M., & Williams, J. B. (1995). *Structured clinical inteview for DSM-IV Axis I disorders*. New York: Biometrics Research Department, Columbia University.

First, M. B., Spitzer, R. L., Girgus, J., & Williams, J. B. (1997a). *Structured clinical interview for DSM Axis I clinican version*. Washington, DC: American Psychiatric Association.

First, M. B., Spitzer, R. L., Girgus, J., & Williams, J. B. (1997b). *Structured clinical interview for DSM Axis II disorders*. New York: Biometrics Research Department, Columbia University.

Frances, A. (2009). Whither DSM-V? *British Journal of Psychiatry, 195*, 391–392.

Frank, E. (2005). *Treating bipolar disorder: A clinician's guide to interpersonal and social rhythm therapy*. New York: Guilford Press.

Freud, S. (1925). Mourning and melancholia. In *Collected Papers* (Vol. 4). London: Hogarth.

Fuchs, C. Z., & Rehm, L. P. (1977). A self control behavior therapy program for depression. *Journal of Consulting and Clinical Psychology, 45*, 206–215.

Greenberg, L., & Watson, J. (2005). *Emotion focused therapy for depression*. Washington, DC: American Psychological Association.

Griner, D., & Smith, T. B. (2006). Culturally adapted mental health intervention: A meta-analytic review. *Psychotherapy: Theory, Research, Practice, Training, 43*, 531–548.

Hamilton, M. (1960). A rating scale for depression. *Journal of Neurology, Neurosurgery, and Psychiatry, 36*, 56–61.

Hamilton, M. (1967). Development of a rating scale for primary depressive illness. *British Journal of School and Clinical Psychology, 6*, 278–296.

Hammen, C. L., & Peters, S. D. (1977). Differential responses to male and female depressive reactions. *Journal of Consulting and Clinical Psychology, 45*, 994–1001.

Hathaway, S. R., & McKinley, J. C. (1951). *MMPI manual (Rev. ed., 1951)*. New York: The Psychological Corporation.

Hautzinger, M., Linden, M., & Hoffman, N. (1982). Distressed couples with and without a depressed partner: An analysis of verbal behavior. *Journal of Behaviour Therapy and Experimental Psychiatry, 13*, 307–314.

Heiby, E. M. (1983). Assessment of frequency of self-reinforcement. *Journal of Personality and Social Psychology, 44*, 1304–1307.

Heppner, P. P., & Petersen, C. H. (1982). The development and implications of a personal problem-solving inventory. *Journal of Counseling Psychology, 29*, 66–75.

Hinchliffe, M., Hooper, D., & Roberts, F. J. (1978). *The melancholy marriage.* New York: Wiley.

Holmes, T. H., & Rahe, R. H. (1967). The social readjustment rating scale. *Journal of Psychosomatic Research, 11*, 213–218.

Hops, H., Biglan, A., Sherman, L., Arthur, J., Friedman, L., & Osteen, V. (1987). Home observations of family interactions of depressed women. *Journal of Consulting and Clinical Psychology, 55*, 341–346.

Hyde, J. S., Mezulis, A. H., & Abramson, L. Y. (2008). The ABCs of depression: Integrating affective, biological, and cognitive models to explain the emergence of the gender difference in depression. *Psychological Review, 115*, 291–313.

Ilardi, S. S. (2009). *The depression cure: The 6-step program to beat depression without drugs.* Cambridge, MA: Da Capo Lifelong Books.

Jacobson, N. S., & Anderson, E. A. (1982). Interpersonal skill and depression in college students: An analysis of the timing of self-disclosures. *Behavior Therapy, 13*, 271–282.

Jacobson, N. S., Dobson, K. S., Truax, P. A., Addis, M. E., Gollan, J. K., Gortner, E., et al. (1996). A component analysis of cognitive-behavioral treatment of depression. *Journal of Consulting and Clinical Psychology, 64*, 295–304.

Kanfer, F. H. (1970). Self-regulation: Research, issues, and speculations. In C. Neuringer & J. L. Michaels (Eds.), *Behavior modification in clinical psychology* (pp. 178–220). New York: Appleton-Century-Crofts.

Kaslow, N. J., McClure, E. B., & Connell, A. M. (2002). Treatment of depression in children and adolescents. In I. H. Gotlib & C. L. Hammen (Eds.), *Handbook of depression* (pp. 441–464). New York: Guilford Press.

Kaslow, N. J., & Racusin, G. R. (1994). Family therapy for depression in young people. In W. M. Reynolds & H. F. Johnston (Eds.), *Handbook of depression in children and adolescents* (pp. 345–363). New York: Plenum Press.

Keller, M. B., McCullough, J. P., Klein, D. N., Arnow, B., Dunner, D. L., Gelenberg, A. J., et al. (2000). A Comparison of nefazodone, the cognitive behavioral-analysis system of psychotherapy, and their combination for the treatment of chronic depression. *New England Journal of Medicine, 342*, 1462–1470.

Kendall, P. C., Howard, B. L., & Hays, R. C. (1989). Self-referent speech and psychopathology: The balance of positive and negative thinking. *Cognitive Therapy and Research, 13*, 583–598.

Kessler, R. C., Berglund, P., Demler, O., Jin, R., Koretz, D., Merikangas, K. R., et al. (2003). The epidemiology of major depressive disorder: results from the National Comorbidity Survey Replication (NCS-R). *Journal of the American Medical Association, 289*, 3095–3105.

Kessler, R. C., Berglund, P., Demler, O., Jin, R., Merikangas, K. R., & Walters, E. E. (2005). Lifetime prevalence and age-of-onset distributions of DSM-IV disorders in the National Comorbidity Survey Replication. *Archives of General Psychiatry, 62*, 593–602.

Kessler, R. C., Chiu, W. T., Demler, O., Merikangas, K. R., & Walters, E. E. (2005). Prevalence, severity, and comorbidity of 12-month DSM-IV disorders in the National Comorbidity Survey Replication. *Archives of General Psychiatry, 62*, 617–627.

Kessler, R. C., McGonagle, K. A., Zhao, S., Nelson, C. B., Hughes, M., Eshleman, S., et al. (1994). Lifetime and 12-month prevalence of DSM-III-R psychiatric disorders in the United States. Results from the National Comorbidity Survey. *Archives of General Psychiatry, 51*, 8–19.

Klerman, G. L., Weissman, M. M., Rounceville, B. J., & Chevron, E. S. (1984). *Interpersonal therapy for depression.* New York: Basic Books.

Klerman, G. L., Weissman, M. M., Rounsaville, B., & Chevron, E. S. (1984). *Interpersonal psychotherapy of depression*. New York: Basic Books.

Kupfer, D. J., Detre, T. P., Foster, F. G., Tucker, G. J., & Delgado, J. (1972). The application of Delgado's telemetric mobility recorder for human studies. *Behavioral Biology, 7*, 585–590.

Kupfer, D. J., & Foster, F. G. (1972). Interval between onset of sleep as an indicator of depression. *Lancet, 2*, 684–686.

Kupfer, D. J., Foster, F. G., Reich, L., Thompson, K. S., & Weiss, B. (1976). EEG sleep changes as predictors of depression. *American Journal of Psychiatry, 133*, 622–626.

Kupfer, D. J., Regier, D. A., & Kuhl, E. A. (2008). On the road to DSM-V and ICD-11. *European Archives of Psychiatry and Clinical Neuroscience, 258*(Supplement 5), 2–6.

Lewinsohn, P. M. (1974). A behavioral approach to depression. In R. J. Friedman & M. M. Katz (Eds.), *The psychology of depression: Contemporary theory and research* (pp. 157–178). New York: Winston/Wiley

Lewinsohn, P. M., Antonuccio, D. O., Steinmetz-Breckenridge, J. L., & Teri, L. (1984). *The coping with depression course: A psychoeducational intervention for unipolar depression*. Eugene, OR: Castalia Publishing.

Lewinsohn, P. M., Biglan, A., & Zeiss, A. M. (1976). Behavioral treatment of depression. In P. O. Davidson (Ed.), *The behavioral management of anxiety, depression and pain* (pp. 91–146). New York: Brunner/Mazel.

Lewinsohn, P. M., & Clarke, G. N. (1999). Psychosocial treatments for adolescent depression. *Clinical Psychology Review, 19*, 329–342.

Lewinsohn, P. M., & Graf, M. (1973). Pleasant activities and depression. *Journal of Consulting and Clinical Psychology, 41*, 261–268.

Lewinsohn, P. M., Hoberman, H. M., Teri, L., & Hautzinger, M. (1985). An integrative theory of depression. In S. Riess & R. R. Bootzin (Eds.), *Theoretical issues in behavior therapy* (pp. 331–359). Orlando, FL: Academic Press.

Lewinsohn, P. M., & Libet, J. (1972). Pleasant events, activity schedules and depression. *Journal of Abnormal Psychology, 79*, 291–295.

Lewinsohn, P. M., & Shaffer, M. (1971). The use of home observation as an integral part of the treatment of depression: Preliminary report and case studies. *Journal of Consulting and Clinical Psychology, 37*, 87–94.

Lewinsohn, P. M., & Shaw, D. A. (1969). Feedback about interpersonal behavior as an agent of behavior change: A case study in the treatment of depression. *Psychotherapy and Psychosomatics, 17*, 82–88.

Lewinsohn, P. M., & Talkington, J. (1979). Studies of the measurement of unpleasant events and relations with depression. *Applied Psychological Measurement, 3*, 83–101.

Lewinsohn, P. M., Weinstein, M. S., & Alper, T. (1970). A behavioral approach to the group treatment of depressed persons: Methodological contribution. *Journal of Clinical Psychology, 26*, 525–532.

Lukoff, D., Liberman, R. P., & Nuechterlein, K. H. (1986). Symptom monitoring in the rehabilitation of schizophrenic patients. *Schizophrenia Bulletin, 12*, 578–602.

MacPhillamy, D. J., & Lewinsohn, P. M. (1971). The pleasant events schedule. Eugene, OR: University of Oregon.

MacPhillamy, D. J., & Lewinsohn, P. M. (1972). *The measurement of reinforcing events*. Paper presented at the 80th annual convention of the APA, Honolulu, HI.

MacPhillamy, D. J., & Lewinsohn, P. M. (1976). Manual for the pleaseant events schedule. Eugene, OR: University of Oregon.

MacPhillamy, D. J., & Lewinsohn, P. M. (1982). The pleasant events schedule: Studies on reliability, validity, and scale intercorrelation. *Journal of Consulting and Clinical Psychology, 50*, 363–380.

Marsella, A. J., Hirschfeld, R. M. A., & Katz, M. M. (Eds.). (1987). *The measurement of depression*. New York: Guilford Press.

Martell, C. R., Addis, M. E., & Jacobson, N. S. (2002). *Depression in context: Strategies for guided action*. New York: W. W. Norton.

Mazzucchelli, T., Kane, R., & Rees, C. (2009). Behavioral activation treatments for depression in adults: A meta-analysis and review. *Clinical Psychology: Science and Practice, 16*, 383–411.

McCullough, J. P. (2000). *Treatment for chronic depression: Cognitive behavioral analysis system of psychotherapy*. New York: Guilford Press.

McLean, P. D., Ogston, K., & Grauer, L. (1973). A behavioral approach to the treatment of depression. *Journal of Behavior Therapy and Experimental Psychiatry, 4*, 323–330.

Merikangas, K. R., Akiskal, H. S., Angst, J., Greenberg, P. E., Hirschfeld, R. M. A., Petukhova, M., et al. (2007). Lifetime and 12-month prevalence of bipolar spectrum disorder in the National Comorbidity Survey replication. *Archives of General Psychiatry, 64*, 543–552.

Millon, T., & Davis, R. D. (1996). *Disorders of personality: DSM-IV and beyond* (rev. ed.). New York: Wiley.

Montgomery, S., & Asberg, M. (1979). A new depression scale designed to be sensitive to change. *American Journal of Psychiatry, 137*, 1081–1084.

Nemeroff, C. B., Heim, C. M., Thase, M. E., Klein, D. N., Rush, A. J., Schatzberg, A. F., et al. (2003). Differential responses to psychotherapy versus pharmacotherapy in patients with chronic forms of major depression and childhood trauma. *Proceedings of the National Academy of Sciences, 100*, 14293–14296.

Nezu, A. M. (1986). Efficacy of a social problem-solving therapy approach for unipolar depression. *Journal of Consulting and Clinical Psychology, 54*, 196–202.

Nezu, A. M., Nezu, C. M., & Perri, M. G. (1989). *Problem solving therapy for depression: Theory, research and clinical guidelines*. New York: Wiley.

Nezu, A. M., & Ronan, G. F. (1985). Life stress, current problems, problem-solving, and depressive symptoms: An integrative model. *Journal of Consulting and Clinical Psychology, 53*, 693–697.

Nezu, A. M., & Ronan, G. F. (1988). Problem solving as a moderator of stress-related depressive symptoms: A prospective analysis. *Journal of Counseling Psychology, 35*, 134–138.

Nezu, A. M., Ronan, G. F., Meadows, E. A., & McClure, K. S. (2000). *Practitioner's guide to empirically based measures of depression*. New York: Kluwer Academic/Plenum Publishers.

Nolen-Hoeksema, S. (1987). Sex differences in unipolar depression: Evidence and theory. *Psychological Bulletin, 101*, 259–282.

Nolen-Hoeksema, S., Girgus, J., & Seligman, M. E. P. (1991). Sex differences in depression and explanatory style in children. *Journal of Youth and Adolescence, 20*, 233–245.

Nolen-Hoeksema, S., Larson, J., & Grayson, C. (1999). Explaining the gender differences in depressive symptoms. *Journal of Personality and Social Psychology, 77*, 1061–1072.

O'Hara, M. W., & Rehm, L. P. (1985). Self-monitoring, activity levels, and mood in the development and maintenance of depression. *Journal of Abnormal Psychology, 88*, 450–453.

O'Hara, M. W., Rehm, L. P., & Campbell, S. B. (1982). Predicting depressive symptomatology: Cognitive behavioral models and postpartum depression. *Journal of Abnormal Psychology, 91*, 457–461.

O'Hara, M. W., Rehm, L. P., & Campbell, S. B. (1983). Postpartum depression: A role for social network and life stress variables. *Journal of Nervous and Mental Disease, 171*, 336–341.

Osgood, C. E. (1962). Studies on the generality of affective meaning systems. *American Psychologist, 17*, 10–28.

Overall, J. E., & Gorman, D. R. (1962). The brief psychiatric rating scale. *Psychological Reports, 10*, 799–812.

Parker, G., & Manicavasagar, V. (2005). *Modeling and managing the depressive disorders: A clinical guide*. Cambridge, UK: Cambridge University Press.

Paykel, E. S., Weissman, M. M., Prusoff, B. A., & Tonks, C. M. (1971). Dimensions of social adjustment in depressed women. *Journal of Nervous and Mental Disease, 152*, 158–172.

Petersen, C. H., Semmel, A., von Bayer, C., Asberg, M., Metalsky, G. I., & Semmel, A. (1982). The Atttributional Style Questionnaire. *Cognitive Therapy and Research, 6,* 287–300.

Pettit, J. W., & Joiner, T. E., Jr. (2005). *The interpersonal solution to depression: A workbook for changing how you feel by changing how you relate.* Oakland, CA: New Harbinger Publications.

Radloff, L. S. (1975). Sex differences in depression: The effects of occupation and marital status. *Sex Roles, 1,* 249–265.

Radloff, L. S. (1977). The CES-D scale: A self-report depression scale for research in the general population. *Applied Psychological Measurement, 1,* 385–401.

Raskin, A., Schulterbrandt, J., Reatig, N., & McKeon, J. J. (1969). Replication of factors of psychopathology in interview, ward behavior, and self-report ratings of hospitalized depressives. *Journal of Nervous and Mental Disease, 148,* 87–98.

Raskin, A., Schulterbrandt, J., Reatig, N., & Rice, C. E. (1967). Factors of psychopathology in interview, ward behavior and self-report ratings of hospitalized depressives. *Journal of Consulting Psychology, 31,* 270–278.

Regier, D. A., Boyd, J. H., Burke, J. D., Jr., Rae, D. S., Myers, J. K., Kramer, M., et al. (1988). One-month prevalence of mental disorders in the United States. Based on five epidemiologic catchment area sites. *Archives of General Psychiatry, 45,* 977–986.

Rehm, L. P. (1977). A self control model of depression. *Behavior Therapy, 8,* 787–804.

Rehm, L. P. (1988). Assessment of depression. In A. S. Bellack & M. Hersen (Eds.), *Behavioral assessment: A practical handbook* (pp. 313–364). New York: Pergamon Press.

Rehm, L. P., & Adams, J. H. (2009). Self-management. In W. O'Donohue & J. Fisher (Eds.), *General principles and empirically supported techniques of cognitive behavioral therapy* (pp. 564–570). New York: Wiley.

Rehm, L. P., Fuchs, C. Z., Roth, D. M., Kornblith, S. J., & Romano, J. (1979). A comparison of self control and social skills treatments of depression. *Behavior Therapy, 10,* 429–442.

Rehm, L. P., & Kaslow, N. J. (1984). Behavioral approaches to depression: Research results and clinical recommendations In C. M. Franks (Ed.), *New developments in behavior therapy* (pp. 155–229). New York: Haworth Press.

Rehm, L. P., Kornblith, S. J., O'Hara, M. W., Lamparski, D. M., Romano, J. M., & Volkin, J. I. (1981). An evaluation of major components in a self control therapy program for depression. *Behavior Modification, 5,* 459–490.

Rehm, L. P., & Naus, M. J. (1990). A memory model of emotion. In R. E. Ingram (Ed.), *Contemporary psychological approaches to depression: Theory, research and treatment* (pp. 23–35). New York: Plenum Publishing.

Rehm, L. P., & O'Hara, M. W. (1985). Item characteristics of the Hamilton Rating Scale for Depression. *Journal of Psychiatric Research, 19,* 31–41.

Robins, L. N., Helzer, J. E., Croughan, J., & Ratcliff, K. S. (1981). National Institute of Mental Health Diagnostic Interview Schedule. Its history, characteristics, and validity. *Archives of General Psychiatry, 38,* 381–389.

Robinson, J. C., & Lewinsohn, P. M. (1973). Behavior modification of speech characteristics in a chornically depressed man. *Behavior Modification, 4,* 150–152.

Rokke, P. D., Tomhave, J. A., & Jocic, Z. (1999). The role of client choice and target selection in self-management therapy for depression in older adults. *Psychology and Aging, 14,* 155–169.

Rosenbaum, M. (1980). A schedule for assessing self-control behaviors: Preliminary findings. *Behavior Therapy, 11,* 109–121.

Rosenbaum, M., & Jaffe, Y. (1983). Learned helplessness: The role of individual differences in learned resourcefulness. *British Journal of Social Psychology, 22,* 215–225.

Rude, S. S., & Rehm, L. P. (1991). Cognitive and behavioral predictors of response to treatments for depression. *Clinical Psychology Review, 11,* 493–514.

Russell, J. A. (1980). A circumplex model of affect. *Journal of Personality and Social Psychology, 39,* 1161–1178.

Segal, Z. V., Williams, J. M. G., & Teasdale, J. D. (2002). *Mindfulness-based cognitive therapy for depression: A new approach to preventing relapse.* New York: Guildford Press.

Seligman, M. E. P. (1981). A learned helplessness point of view. In L. P. Rehm (Ed.), *Behavior therapy for depression: Present status and future directions* (pp. 123–142). New York: Academic Press.

Seligman, M. E. P. (1990). Why is there so much depression today? The waxing of the individual and the waning of the commons. In R. E. Ingram (Ed.), *Contemporary psychological approaches to depression: Theory, research and treatment* (pp. 1–9). New York: Plenum Press.

Seligman, M. E. P., Abramson, L. Y., Semmel, A., & von Bayer, C. (1979). Depressive attributional style. *Journal of Abnormal Psychology, 88,* 242–247.

Seligman, M. E. P., Schulman, P., DeRubeis, R. J., & Hollon, S. D. (1999). The prevention of depression and anxiety. *Prevention and Treatment, 2,* ArtID 8a.

Shaffer, D., Fisher, P., Dulcan, M. K., Davies, M., Piacentini, J., Schwab-Stone, M. E., et al. (1996). The NIMH diagnostic interview schedule for children version 2.3 (DISC-2.3): Description, acceptability, prevalence rates, and performance in the MECA study. *Journal of the American Academy of Child & Adolescent Psychiatry, 35,* 865–877.

Shipley, C. R., & Fazio, A. F. (1973). Pilot study of a treatment for psychological depression. *Journal of Abnormal Psychology, 82,* 372–376.

Spitzer, R. L., Endicott, J., & Robins, E. (1975). Research diagnostic criteria. *Psychopharmalogia Bulletin, 11,* 22–25.

Spitzer, R. L., Endicott, J., & Robins, E. (1978). Research diagnostic criteria: Rationale and reliability. *Archives of General Psychiatry, 36,* 773–782.

Stark, K. D. (1990). *Childhood depression: School based intervention.* New York: Guilford Press.

Thase, M. E., Friedman, E. S., Biggs, M. M., Wisniewski, S. R., Trivedi, M. H., Luther, J. F., et al. (2007). Cognitive therapy versus medication in augmentation and switch strategies as second-step treatments: A STAR*D report. *American Journal of Psychiatry, 164,* 739–752.

Thombs, B. D., de Jonge, P., Coyne, J. C., Whooley, M. A., Frasure-Smith, N., Mitchell, A. J., et al. (2008). Depression screening and patient outcomes in cardiovascular care: A systematic review. *Journal of the American Medical Association, 300,* 2161–2171.

Thompson, L. W., Gallagher, D., & Breckenridge, J. S. (1987). Comparative effectiveness of psychotherapies for depressed elders. *Journal of Consulting and Clinical Psychology, 55,* 385–390.

Twenge, J., & Nolen-Hoeksema, S. (2002). Age, gender, race, socioeconomic status, and birth cohort differences in the Children's Depression Inventory: A meta-analysis. *Journal of Abnormal Psychology, 111,* 578–588.

US Department of Health and Human Services. (2001). *Mental health: Culture, race and ethnicity - A supplement to mental health: A report of the surgeon general - Executive summary.* Rockville, MD: US Department of Health and Human Services, Public Health Service, Office of the Surgeon General.

Vittengl, J. R., Clark, L. A., Dunn, T. W., & Jarrett, R. B. (2007). Reducing relapse and recurrence in unipolar depression: a comparative meta-analysis of cognitive-behavioral therapy's effects. *Journal of Consulting and Clinical Psychology, 75,* 475–488.

Watson, D., Clark, L. A., & Tellegen, A. (1988). Development and validation of brief measures of positive and negative affect: The PANAS scales. *Journal of Personality and Social Psychology, 54,* 1063–1070.

Watson, D., & Tellegen, A. (1985). Toward a consensual structure of mood. *Psychological Bulletin, 98,* 219–235.

Waxer, P. (1976). Nonverbal cues for depression: Set versus no set. *Journal of Consulting and Clinical Psychology, 44,* 493.

Weissman, A. N., & Beck, A. T. (1978). *Development and validation of the Dysfunctional Attitudes Scale: A preliminary investigation.* Paper presented at the annual meeting of the Association for the Advancement of Behavior Therapy, Chicago, IL.

Weissman, M. M., Bland, R., Canino, G., Fararvelli, C., Greenwald, S., Hwu, H., et al. (1996). Cross-national epidemiology of major depression and bipolar disorder. *Journal of the American Medical Association, 276*, 293–299.

Weissman, M. M., & Klerman, G. L. (1977). Sex differences in the epidemiology of depression. *Archives of General Psychiatry, 34*, 98–111.

Williams, J. G., Barlow, D. H., & Agras, W. S. (1972). Behavioral measurement of severe depression. *Archives of General Psychiatry, 27*, 330–333.

Wing, J. K. (1970). A standard form of psychiatric present state examination. In E. H. Hare & J. K. Wing (Eds.), *Psychiatric epidemiology* (pp. 93–131). London: Oxford University Press.

Winokur, G., & Clayton, P. (1967). Family history studies: II. Sex differences and alchoholism in primary affective illness. *British Journal of Psychiatry, 113*, 973–979.

Wolpe, J. (1958). *Psychotherapy by reciprocal inhibition*. Stanford, CA: Stanford University Press.

World Health Organization. (1992). *International statistical classification of diseases and related health problems. Tenth revision*. Geneva: World Health Organization.

Yost, E. B., Beutler, L. E., Corbishley, M. A., & Allender, J. R. (1986). *Group cognitive therapy: A treatment approach for depressed older adults*. New York: Pergamon Books.

Youngren, M. A., & Lewinsohn, P. M. (1980). The functional relationship between depression and problematic interpersonal behavior. *Journal of Abnormal Psychology, 89*, 333–341.

Zeiss, A. M., Lewinsohn, P. M., & Muñoz, R. F. (1979). Nonspecific improvement effects in depression using interpersonal skills training, pleasant activity schedules, or cognitive training. *Journal of Consulting and Clinical Psychology, 47*, 427–439.

Zettle, R. D., Haflich, J. L., & Reynolds, R. A. (2006). Responsivity to cognitive therapy as a function of treatment format and client personality. *Journal of Clinical Psychology, 48*, 787–797.

Zimmerman, M., Coryell, W., Corenthal, C., & Wilson, S. (1986). A self-report scale to diagnose major depressive disorder. *Archives of General Psychiatry, 43*, 1076–1081.

Zimmerman, M., Sheeran, T., & Young, D. (2004). The Diagnostic Inventory for Depression: A self-report scale to diagnose DSM-IV major depressive disorder. *Journal of Clinical Psychology, 60*, 87–110.

Zung, W. W. K. (1965). A self-rating depression scale. *Archives of General Psychiatry, 12*, 63–70.

Zung, W. W. K. (1974). *The measurement of depression*. Milwaukee: Lakeside Laboratories.

Zuroff, D. C., Quinlan, D. M., & Blatt, S. J. (1990). Psychometric properties of the Depressive Experiences Questionnaire in a college population. *Journal of Personality Assessment, 55*, 65–72.

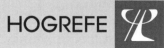

Christoph Flückiger, Günther Wüsten, Richard E. Zinbarg, Bruce E. Wampold

Resource Activation
Using Clients' Own Strengths in Psychotherapy and Counseling

2010, viii + 70 pages, US $ 24.80 / € 17.95, ISBN: 978-0-88937-378-5

This concise practice-oriented manual effectively shows how psychologists, psychiatrists, social workers, supervisors, and counselors can quickly identify and put to therapeutic use an individual's own talents and resources.

Written in an easy and relaxed style using everyday language, this manual illustrates how to actively take a person's resources into consideration during therapy and counseling sessions, and how to integrate them into existing intervention concepts.

The first part illustrates approaches that can be used to focus attention on assessment and dialog, and that shed light on a person's individual resources from various angles. These therapeutic approaches can be used in the framework of existing manuals and guidelines to focus on how to "do things."

The second part illustrates procedures offering a framework for further applying the different perspectives and provides sample worksheets for practical use.

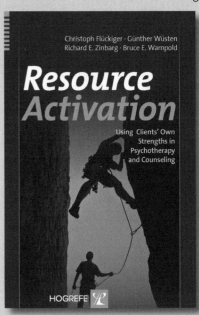

"Resource Activation *heralds the emergence of a new vista for psychotherapists. It provides a detailed roadmap for systemically assessing and utilizing clients' talents, skills, and resources to facilitate therapeutic change. It gives very specific therapeutic guidelines and also lays the foundation for research on this historically neglected area. This book and this work should be read and utilized by individual, couple, and family therapists to realistically enhance their clients' sense of self and relationship efficacy"*

William M. Pinsof, PhD, President, The Family Institute, Northwestern University, Evanston, IL, USA

Table of Contents

For further details visit **www.hogrefe.com**

Order online at: **www.hogrefe.com** or call toll-free **(800) 228-3749**

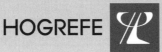 **HOGREFE**

Hogrefe Publishing · 30 Amberwood Parkway · Ashland, OH 44805
Tel: (800) 228 3749 · Fax: (419) 281 6883 · E-Mail: custserv@hogrefe.com
Hogrefe Publishing · Rohnsweg 25 · 37085 Göttingen, Germany
Tel: +49 551 999 500 · Fax: +49 551 999 50 425 · E-Mail: custserv@hogrefe.de